Equity Flex Options:
The Financial Engineer's Most Versatile Tool

James J. Angel
Georgetown University

Gary L. Gastineau
American Stock Exchange

Clifford J. Weber
American Stock Exchange

Published by Frank J. Fabozzi Associates

Cover design by Scott C. Riether

 © 1999 By Frank J. Fabozzi Associates
New Hope, Pennsylvania

ISBN: 1-883249-58-9

Printed in the United States of America

Table of Contents

Acknowledgments

Sections of various chapters have appeared previously as part of the following works:

Angel, James J., Gary L. Gastineau, and Clifford J. Weber, "Using Exchange-Traded Equity FLEX Put Options in Corporate Stock Repurchase Programs," *Journal of Applied Corporate Finance*, Vol. 10, No.1, Spring 1997, pp. 109-113.

Angel, James J., Gary L. Gastineau, and Clifford J. Weber, "A New Trade Implementation and Portfolio Management Tool for Institutional Investors: Exchange-Traded Stock Options," *Derivatives Quarterly*, Vol. 4, No. 2, Winter 1997, pp. 26-35.

Angel, James J., Gary L. Gastineau, and Clifford J. Weber, "Reducing the Market Impact of Large Stock Trades," *The Journal of Portfolio Management* (Fall 1997), pp. 69-76.

Angel, James J., Gary L. Gastineau, and Clifford J. Weber, "Flexible Friends," *Risk*, Vol.10, No. 10, pp. 40-45.

Gastineau, Gary L., "A Changing Perspective on Teaching Options," *Financial Practice and Education*, Vol. 7, No. 2, Fall/Winter 1997, pp. 89-93.

Gastineau, Gary L., *The Options Manual* (New York: McGraw-Hill, 1988).

Chapter 1

Introduction

The Swiss Army Knife is a classic metaphor for the universal tool. The owner of a full-featured Swiss Army Knife can slice, saw, punch, cut, uncap, screw or unscrew, trim, or even uncork just about anything. Equity FLEX options have much the same degree of versatility in the hands of a skilled financial artisan. As a tool, however, Equity FLEX options are a cut above the Swiss Army Knife. The Swiss Army Knife is rarely the best tool for a specific application; its virtues are versatility and convenience. By contrast, the Equity FLEX option is often the best available tool for the purposes of the financial engineer and the investor he serves.

An Equity FLEX option is an option contract with some customized terms. It is traded on a regulated options exchange and cleared and guaranteed by the Options Clearing Corporation (OCC). It is available on common stocks eligible for standardized option trading and many Index Share products.[1] The customized terms can include the option's strike price, expiration date, and exercise style (European or American). This book consolidates and extends a number of papers we have written on Equity FLEX options applications to illustrate how Equity FLEX options can solve a surprisingly wide range of risk, tax, and trading problems that have eluded cost-effective solutions in the past. Indeed, Equity FLEX options can solve previously intractable financial problems.

---

[1] Index Shares — including SPDRs, MidCap SPDRs, DIAMONDS and WEBS — are stock portfolio or basket securities designed to track certain benchmark indices. They are listed for trading on the American Stock Exchange and offer the opportunity to buy and sell a fund or fund-like security throughout the trading day and to create and redeem shares daily at Net Asset Value (NAV). More detailed information on specific Index Share funds is available in each product's prospectus. A user-friendly summary of the key features of the S&P 500 SPDRs is in James J. Angel, Don M. Chance, Jack Clark Francis, and Gary L. Gastineau, "Comparison of Two Low-Cost S&P 500 Index Funds," *Derivatives Quarterly* (Spring 1996), pp. 32-38.

Our focus is on problem solving, but a very brief introductory description of how Equity FLEX option transactions work is a necessary prelude to a discussion of a number of financial market problems where Equity FLEX options can be part or all of the solution. In the last chapter of this book we provide a detailed user's manual for Equity FLEX options. Our suggested applications combined with more widespread knowledge of Equity FLEX opportunities in the financial community should lead to more active and more liquid option markets and to the development of even more uses for these versatile tools.

It is useful to keep in mind that opportunities for large scale use of exchange-traded options were severely limited before late 1997. Prior to that time, the position limits, transaction costs, and inflexible terms of traditional exchange-traded options made it difficult for large institutional investors to use exchange-traded options. The Equity FLEX option is central to a number of changes in market structure which now make large scale option trades feasible. These initial changes need to be extended by development of an application infrastructure before many of the Equity FLEX solutions we describe can be pursued on a large scale. The application discussions will clarify the substantial incentives that will encourage investment banks and other service providers to create the necessary infrastructure.

We recognize that not every reader will care about every topic we cover in this book. Consumers of transaction services or structured products may be satisfied with simple descriptions of a few applications that interest them. Suppliers of transaction services and equity investment products will find the development of infrastructure and the interaction between various applications of greatest interest. Option and stock traders and operations managers will be interested in the Equity FLEX trading and support mechanisms. We have tried to break the text into clearly marked segments so readers can find what they need. We have not duplicated widely available discussions of topics like option valuation, volatility estimation, risk management or option payout patterns unless the context requires a more detailed explanation of some point. Our focus is primarily on issues that have not mattered and opportunities that have not been available in the "pre-revolution" option market.

REVOLUTIONARY CHANGES IN THE OPTIONS MARKETS

Since 1996, three developments have occurred which open the U.S. options markets to large scale options users for the first time. On October 24, 1996, the American Stock Exchange and several other exchanges introduced Equity FLEX options trading on a small group of listed option stocks. In subsequent months, additional names were added regularly to the initial list of Equity FLEX eligible stocks. Any stock that meets SEC requirements for standardized option trading can be added to the list in response to investor demand.

While this book is about Equity FLEX options, the introduction of flexible option terms is probably less important than two other changes that occurred within the first year of Equity FLEX trading. In September 1997, the Securities and Exchange Commission approved complete elimination of Equity FLEX position limits in response to a request from the American Stock Exchange.[2] Subject to relatively modest liquidity concerns, major institutional investors can now take option positions of substantial size in pursuit of a variety of trading and investment objectives. In an earlier step to encourage large investors to use options, the American Stock Exchange announced a cap on option transaction charges effective June 2, 1997.

These three developments:

- the introduction of the Equity FLEX trading structure,
- the elimination of position limits for Equity FLEX options, and
- the capping of American Stock Exchange transaction charges for all large options transactions

make exchange-traded options accessible and attractive to large scale investors for the first time. The significance of these structural changes, separately and in combination, is developed at length in the next chapter. In summary, these changes have made large-scale institutional use of exchange-traded options legal, feasible and economically interesting for the first time. The applications described in this book and many

---

[2] The SEC had initially approved position limits covering purchase or sale of Equity FLEX options on up to 7,500,000 underlying shares on some large cap, actively traded stocks.

others that will develop over time promise to change the options markets — and the markets in underlying stocks. The feasibility of large scale options transactions will eventually change the perspectives of all investors, whether they use options themselves or simply enjoy the benefits of greater use of options in the securities markets.

LARGE SCALE OPTIONS APPLICATIONS

Under appropriate application headings, we will describe how institutions and other large equity market participants can find solutions to a variety of problems. We will describe options applications to:

- Reduce market impact from the sale or purchase of a large block of stock.

- Facilitate portfolio cash management and risk management by separating stock market risk from the size of a cash commitment.

- Create synthetic long positions that may provide better returns than an outright stock purchase:
  - With a synthetic stock position a non-U.S. investor can side-step the dividend withholding tax.
  - A fixed income manager can offer an equity portfolio overlay on an enhanced money market return.

- Create synthetic short positions with greater protection from buy-ins and/or lower net carrying costs than traditional short positions.

- Permit investors to use more of the research information that they develop from company, industry, or market analyses. They can do this with Equity FLEX by profiting from volatility forecasts or by structuring payout patterns to reflect more sophisticated forecasts than the simple "up or down" price forecast which underlies most stock portfolio selections. These applications involve event and earnings surprise risk management opportunities.

- Accept some risks and hedge others in risk arbitrage situations.

- Increase the flexibility of corporations that sell puts as part of their stock repurchase programs.

- Permit investors to value the voting rights attached to shares separately from the other investment characteristics of the shares.

- Let creditors — or even the corporate treasury — buy out-of-the-money puts as protection from corporate default.

These specific applications are described in more detail in Chapters 3-5. Some of the applications are clearly important and some seem almost trivial at first glance. Our justification for offering a wide range of suggested uses is that an application that seems unimportant to most of us may be crucial to a specific user. The range of applications described is deliberately broad to stimulate readers to develop their own ideas. Many new applications will come from innovative investors examining the features of what is, in effect, an entirely new financial market.

Many press accounts of Equity FLEX developments have described this new market as a challenge to the OTC options market. Actually, competition between OTC and exchange-traded option markets has not been significant. With the exception of the sale of puts in corporate stock repurchase programs, where Equity FLEX should ultimately replace the OTC product, these markets are not likely to be significant competitors. To appreciate this viewpoint, the reader needs to understand the significance of Equity FLEX in what we call the institutional options revolution.

Chapter 2

The Institutional
Options Revolution

Three recent changes in U.S. options markets promise dramatic increases in options use by institutional investors. The introduction of Equity FLEX options is probably the least important of the three, but Equity FLEX made the other changes possible — and probably inevitable.

FLEXIBLE TERMS FROM EQUITY FLEX OPTIONS

Equity FLEX options are identical in many respects to the standardized options which have been traded on national securities exchanges and have been cleared and collateralized by the Options Clearing Corporation for 25 years. In contrast to standardized options, however, Equity FLEX options permit significant contract customization by the parties to the trade. Specifically, Equity FLEX put options can have non-standard strike prices and all Equity FLEX options can have non-standard expiration dates and expiration styles (European or American).[1] Until a relatively arcane tax issue can be resolved, Equity FLEX call options will trade only with standard strikes.[2] Other fine tuning adjustments may be added from time to time, as the market in Equity FLEX options continues to evolve.

---

[1] A European-style option can be exercised only on its expiration date. An American-style option can be exercised on any business day prior to and including the expiration date.

[2] See the discussion, "When will it be possible to customize call strike prices?" in Appendix B. Under current Exchange and OCC rules, the flexibility of put strike prices is greater than the flexibility of call strike prices. If standard strike prices for calls are not satisfactory, the parties to the transaction could use European put-call parity to create a synthetic call. Readers unfamiliar with European put-call parity may find the discussions of put-call parity and synthetic stock in Chapter 5 of particular interest.

Equity FLEX options pricing is determined by open outcry on the Exchange floor. In contrast to OTC options where an investor usually negotiates with a single dealer, the Equity FLEX participant can obtain an initial pricing indication from a dealer of his or her choice, followed by exposure of the proposed transaction in the market and the opportunity for the exchange specialist, market makers, off-floor dealers, and/or investors to provide better terms than the original dealer (who takes the trade to the Exchange floor and manages the order) has been able to offer. The result of this price discovery process will be transaction terms no worse — and possibly much better — than the proposal of the original dealer because the trade may fit someone else's needs far better than it fits the dealer's ability to accommodate the customer. The dealer acts as the customer's agent in getting the best possible terms on the trade and can participate in part or all of the trade depending on how the transaction fits his book. The AAA credit rating of the Options Clearing Corporation, the counterparty on all exchange-traded options, eliminates any concern about an OTC option dealer's credit rating.

NO POSITION LIMITS ON EQUITY FLEX OPTIONS

At least as important as the flexible terms available on Equity FLEX options is that in September 1997, the SEC approved the complete elimination of position limits on Equity FLEX contracts — subject to some surveillance requirements which are primarily the concern of brokers, the Exchange, and the Options Clearing Corporation.

The complete elimination of position limits is critically important for the development of institutional option applications. In the options market environment which prevailed for most of the first quarter century of listed options trading, major institutional investors found it economically impractical to use stock options because the largest position any investors could take would not have a material impact on their large portfolios. With the elimination of position limits on Equity FLEX options, the greatest obstacle to large-scale options use has been removed and a wide-range of institutions will be able to use options for the first time.

When exchange-listed option began trading in 1973, a last minute rule change imposed position limits of 1,000 contracts (100,000 underlying shares) on any investor or group acting in concert. Position limits were liberalized in subsequent years, but the expansion in position limits barely kept ahead of a rising stock market because stock splits kept the average stock price among large capitalization stocks close to the 1973 level. The elimination of Equity FLEX position limits was followed in 1998 by a tripling of position limits on standard options. The American Stock Exchange will continue to press for the elimination of all option position limits. Based on the fact that elimination of position limits on Equity-FLEX did not cause chaos in financial markets and on the importance of some of the applications described in Chapters 3-5, this campaign should be successful.

REDUCTION IN EXCHANGE TRANSACTION CHARGES ON LARGE TRANSACTIONS

A secondary obstacle to large scale transactions in options has been the fixed per contract exchange transaction charges which were prevalent until recently. In June 1997, the American Stock Exchange capped its customer transaction charges at 2,000 contracts on all equity and index option contracts. Before this cap went into effect, a customer trading a stock option contract priced at more than $1.00 per underlying share would pay an exchange fee, clearance fee, and exchange floor brokerage fee totaling $0.37 per contract no matter how many contracts were part of the transaction. A customer's purchase or sale of 100,000 contracts would carry Exchange fees of $37,000. A purchase *and* a sale would carry fees of $74,000. Under the AMEX's transaction charge cap, exchange fees now are charged only on the first 2,000 contracts of a transaction. In this example, the customer exchange fees would be a maximum of $740 on one side of a trade no matter how large the transaction. Other exchanges offer some discounts on larger transactions; but, as of this writing, only the AMEX has capped fees.

The Options Clearing Corporation has begun experimenting with lower per contract clearing fees in response to growing options volume. The current OCC fee schedule which caps clearing fees at

2,000 contracts is reproduced in Exhibit 10 in Chapter 6. The trend is clearly in the direction of recognizing that large fees without a quantity discount are not effective for the simple reason that if a trade does not occur on an exchange because fees are too high, there is no opportunity to collect *any* revenue from the trade.

STRATEGIES VERSUS TACTICS — CHANGING THE IMAGE OF OPTIONS IN PORTFOLIO MANAGEMENT

Clearly, the introduction of customized Equity FLEX contract terms, the elimination of position limits in this market sector, and capped fees on the Exchange are important changes, but potential users also need to see options in a new light. Long calls, short puts, spreads, straddles and strangles, as well as collars, seagulls and Christmas trees are invariably called *options strategies*. This terminology goes back to the conventional or over-the-counter options market that preceded exchange-traded options. We live in an era of strategic planning, strategic weapons, and strategies for success. Inevitably, we try to wrap the connotations of "strategy" around some non-strategic things.

In a military context, commanders refer to large-scale planning or global activities as strategic. Smaller scale actions taken to implement a strategy usually fall under the heading of "tactics." The relevance of this distinction to options is that, perhaps as much as any other single factor, the use of the word "strategy" in connection with options has led some investors and pedagogues to focus too much on the theory of options, on option valuation, and on the aggregate impact of options on portfolio performance — and too little on tactical options applications. The introduction of Equity FLEX options offers an opportunity to redress the balance.

If options are strategic, it is too easy to see them as inherently more important than the underlying instrument. We can lose sight of the risk/reward characteristics of an unoptioned portfolio if we use options to change the risk/reward pattern drastically. Focusing on an option strategy's payout pattern rather than on the usefulness of an option application, may be akin to a military commander choosing his weapons before he learns the nature of his mission. It is probably easier to view Equity FLEX options from a tactical perspective than it is to attain this perspective with index options which inherently affect the risk/return characteristics of an entire portfolio. Tactical option applications not only address the importance of thinking small in terms of position or portfolio impact, they also extend the usefulness of options to problems often ignored by big-picture users of options.

We still need to understand option valuation; but, increasingly, the emphasis will be on integrating option valuation with the economics of other applications. These applications include trading cost reduction, asset allocation, return pattern adjustment, utility enhancement, and cost of capital reduction. In a number of these applications, buyers or sellers of an option may be willing to buy or sell a somewhat mispriced option to accomplish some other objective. The acceptability of some mispricing in a stock option may be the best indication that the option is being used as a tactical tool. As the reader will see when reading the discussion of Equity FLEX applications which follows, our emphasis is more on tactics than on strategy. The reader should also note that many of these applications will be possible with standard options as position limits rise and ultimately disappear.

Chapter 3

Applications of Equity FLEX Options

T his chapter introduces many useful applications of Equity FLEX options. Most of these applications will work with standard options, but some require the special terms and freedom from position limits that is, so far, unique with Equity FLEX. We emphasize once again that these applications are illustrative, not exhaustive. One of our hopes is that these suggestions will stimulate extensions and entirely new directions in the development of option applications.

REDUCING THE MARKET IMPACT FROM THE SALE OF A LARGE BLOCK OF STOCK

A relatively simple example illustrates one market impact reducing application of Equity FLEX options. Suppose that a portfolio manager notes with satisfaction that his position in Technomarvel, Inc. common stock has performed very well in recent months, contributing to the manager's outperformance of his benchmark index. In spite of (or perhaps because of) this recent record, the manager now feels that the stock is not likely to continue its outperformance over the intermediate term. At current prices he would like to replace the stock with a position that is more likely to outperform the benchmark in the months ahead.

A key thing to remember is that an offer to buy or sell sends a signal about the investor's information set. Often this signaling moves the price against an investor, which is known as market impact. For example, an offer to buy stock usually indicates that the buyer expects it to go up. However, the signal does not indicate

13

whether the buyer expects the stock to go up very quickly over a long period of time. An offer to buy a call option sends a more sophisticated signal. The buyer believes that the stock will go up within a fixed time interval, and/or that the stock will be more volatile. Sophisticated traders can reduce market impact by using Equity FLEX options to fine tune the signals they send with their orders.

The logistics of selling the Technomarvel position outright without substantial market impact are daunting. The manager's portfolios own 10 million shares with a current market value of approximately $500 million — not an uncommon position in institutional portfolios. If the institution's trader simply indicates interest in selling a block of this size, any corresponding buying interest is likely to be well below the currently quoted bid.[1]

Any investor who is a candidate for purchase of all or a substantial fraction of a half billion dollar block of stock recognizes that the sell decision may be based on specific adverse information. The seller may know, or think he knows, something that makes the stock a dangerous holding for the period ahead. The possibility of an earnings disappointment or of bad news affecting the company's product line or its sales could cause the shares to underperform — or even to fall sharply. The possibility that such information is behind the decision to sell makes any potential buyer reluctant to purchase the block, except at a significant discount. *In a traditional stock transaction, the seller has no obvious way to assure the buyer that the decision to sell is not based on this kind of information.*

Equity FLEX options provide a simple way to send a signal — and even to offer *an enforceable "guarantee"* — that the seller does not have stock specific information that could hurt the buyer. The trader for the selling institution can indicate that, as an alternative to selling the shares outright, the fund is willing to sell calls with a strike price near the current market price of the stock. The calls are sold in the expectation that the option will be exercised if the stock price moves up (or is unchanged) over the life of the option.

---

[1] The seller may be able to sell a small quantity of the stock through a crossing network or similar system, but even such anonymous sales will soon begin to have an impact on the stock price.

Figure 1: Holding Stock Outright versus Selling a Call on the Stock

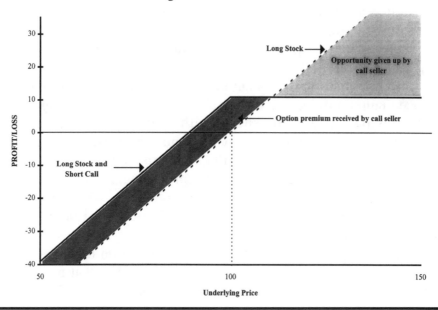

What better way to indicate the absence of adverse information than to offer a potential buyer a call option on the shares? Whether the would-be buyer elects to buy the call options (perhaps priced at a modest discount in implied volatility points to the price of standardized exchange-traded options) or simply makes a more competitive bid for the stock in reliance on the option offer, the fact that the alternative was available sends a signal to any buyer that the sale is not based on adverse information. The buyer of the call option knows that if the stock declines over the life of the option, the seller will collect an option premium. However, any loss on the stock greater than the amount of the option premium can affect the seller's portfolio significantly. If the stock is simply dull, as the seller anticipated, he collects the option premium. His view on the stock suggests that even the reduced premium will probably make the stock and option combination a better contributor to portfolio performance than it would have been without the option. If the stock is above the strike at expiration, the seller will succeed in moving the block with negligible market impact. Figure 1 shows the profit/

loss effect of this approach to liquidating a large position from the seller's perspective. The darkly shaded area is the option premium received and the lightly shaded area is the opportunity loss if the stock rises in price after the call is sold.

The decision to buy the option rather than the stock will be based on such issues as the expected cash flow into and out of the buyer's portfolio, his fund's authorization to purchase call options, his judgment on the likely future volatility of the underlying stock, and, of course, the credibility of the statement implied by the option offer. If he feels the stock price will be more unstable than the level of volatility discounted by the option premium he is asked to pay, he may elect to purchase the option as a preferred alternative to direct purchase of the stock — even if he believes the seller has no adverse information. Figure 2 illustrates the tradeoffs the would-be stock buyer makes by purchasing the call rather than buying the stock outright. The medium shaded area shows the premium the buyer pays for the call. The darkly shaded area shows the value of the loss protection the call provides if the stock drops and the lightly shaded area shows the call buyer's upside participation after deducting the premium paid for the call.

Figure 2: Buying Stock versus Buying a Call

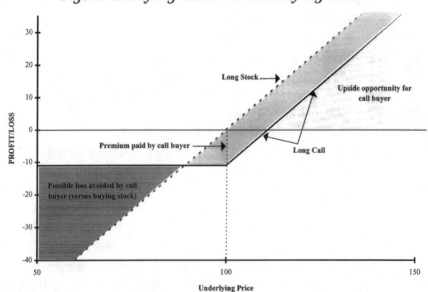

The would-be seller still owns the stock for a significant period after selling the call. We noted at the outset of this discussion that the manager is comfortable with the stock's delayed sale and with the downside exposure he has until the option is exercised, but we need to address the issue of the fund's exposure in a rising market. A fund selling a number of large positions subject to the exercise of calls will behave quite differently from its more traditional competitors, particularly in a strongly rising market. Some managers will not be concerned with such differences; others will want to buy calls on a potential replacement stock or otherwise modify the portfolio. The range of possibilities is beyond our current topic, but portfolio managers need to consider the issue.

SELLING A PUT TO BUY STOCK —
A STRATEGY FOR THE PATIENT BUYER

Option-based block trading opportunities are not limited to calls or to stock sales. We can reduce the market impact of a stock *purchase* by selling an Equity FLEX put. These option-facilitated block transactions are on opposite sides of the market, but they have an important characteristic in common: they provide a mechanism to reduce total transaction costs for the investor who is trading on statistical research rather than event-specific knowledge or belief. The option provides a way for this investor to signal and even "guarantee" the level and nature of the conviction behind the decision to trade.

Selling a put to facilitate a possible stock purchase may be useful when an investor decides that a company's shares are undervalued — and may well stay that way for a period of time. Our investor is interested in taking and holding a position in the stock if the position can be acquired on favorable terms. He expects the values he sees to be reflected in the market price eventually, but not necessarily right away. The stock is attractive at current or lower levels, but the manager cannot justify the purchase if entering a buy order will cause the stock to trade up. In contrast to a traditional buy order which communicates very few nuances, sale of a put may express just the degree of interest and patience which the would-be buyer feels. Adjustments in the option premium, strike price, or expiration date of the put can refine the expression of buying interest.

In emphasizing the possible role of the options market in purchases and sales of blocks of stock, we do not mean to imply that there will be no market impact from a stock purchase or sale decision implemented with options. The purchase or sale of options in large size will almost certainly have some impact on option premiums and on underlying stock prices. The sale of an at-the-money put indicates buying interest at present or lower prices. This expression of buying interest may prevent a price decline or even stimulate a modest price advance as other buyers see an indication of buying "support." Of course, dealer participation on the other side of a customer's option trade will have stock price impact when the dealer trades in stock to hedge his option position. The dealer's impact is likely to be less than trading the stock outright, however, because hedge ratios are nearly always less than one.

Use of options in block trading should help reduce stock price volatility in some cases. The investor who sells a put will send a message to the market that the stock purchase intention reflected in the put sale is certainly not based on an expectation that a particular event will cause the price of the stock to rise sharply in the period immediately ahead. Instead, the put seller is giving the put buyer most or all of any near term upside in an associated long stock position. The seller of the put is accepting downside exposure to the stock price in exchange for the option premium. If the put seller's judgment is correct, the options will be exercised when the put is slightly in the money. The stock will then rise to reflect the value that this patient investor is looking for.

Figure 3 illustrates the tactical tradeoffs associated with a put sale as a prelude to stock purchase. The darkly shaded area shows the net option premium the put seller will receive after paying for the stock if the stock rises less than the put premium or falls over the life of the put. The lightly shaded area shows the opportunity lost by not buying the stock outright if the stock rises by more than the put premium over the life of the option.

Figure 3: Selling a Put versus Buying Stock Outright

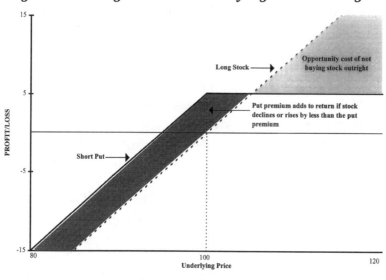

Traders continually wrestle with the difficulty of communicating the strength or weakness of a purchase or sale decision to the market. The party on the other side of the market cannot safely accept a simple statement that the party initiating an order has no specific knowledge of coming events. However, willingness to sell a put as an alternative to immediate purchase of the stock or willingness to sell a call against a long stock position is an eloquent *and enforceable* statement of the option seller's lack of the kind of specific information which is likely to affect the stock price in the short run.

Analysts of trading costs often describe and evaluate the demand for execution immediacy in terms of options.[2] They describe the entry of a limit order to buy or sell a stock as giving other market participants a free option to sell stock to or buy stock from the party entering the limit order. Of course, the option given by the limit order may be exercised after an event has made the bid or offer more attractive — because the option offered by the limit order may be suddenly "in the money." The sale of an exchange-traded call to initiate a stock sale and the sale

---

[2] This approach appears to have originated in Thomas E. Copeland and Dan Galai, "Information Effects on the Bid-Ask Spread," *The Journal of Finance* (December 1983), pp. 1457-1469. A well-developed option analysis of limit orders appears in Evan Schulman, "Shackled Liquidity: An Institutional Manifesto," *Journal of Portfolio Management* (Summer 1992), pp. 42-46.

of a put as a way to begin the process of taking a long position in a stock are simply more explicit uses of options. The limit order that is built into an exchange-traded option is good for a defined interval — the life of the option — in contrast to a simple limit order that is subject to cancellation at the discretion of the party entering the limit order. The explicit sale of an Equity FLEX option also differs from the free options granted by investors using limit orders: the investor selling an Equity FLEX option is paid a cash premium for the option she grants. No cash premium is paid the investor who enters a simple limit order.

CREATING A SYNTHETIC LONG POSITION TO AVOID THE DIVIDEND WITHHOLDING TAX

Equity FLEX options, like standard options, provide non-U.S. investors with an opportunity to side-step the U.S. dividend withholding tax. Although we will touch on exceptions when we examine this technique in more detail in Chapter 5, non-resident (foreign) investors, whether income from their accounts is taxable or tax free in their home country, almost invariably pay a non-recoverable withholding tax on dividends they receive from U.S. stocks. U.S. investors face similar taxes when they invest in other countries, so our examples apply to nearly all cross border investors. If the investor is resident in a tax treaty country, the net withholding tax rate after a partial recovery is typically 15%. If the investor resides in a non-treaty country, the rate is 30%. A 2% yield to an investor in a 15% (treaty) country will generate a 30 basis point annual withholding tax. Table 1 shows the potential annual savings that foreign investors may receive by avoiding the U.S. withholding tax with a synthetic long stock position.

Table 1: U.S. Withholding Tax Savings Possible with Equity Derivatives (basis points)

Dividend Yield:	1%	2%	3%
Net Withholding Tax Rate			
15%-Tax Treaty	15	30	45
30%-Non Tax Treaty	30	60	90

The appropriate calculation of dividend withholding savings in a specific case is based on the period the derivatives position is outstanding. If the position has a life of 30 days and there is no dividend paid during that period, then no credit for saving dividend withholding taxes is attributable to the synthetic stock position. If, on the other hand, a 30 day position covers an ex-dividend date, the value of the withholding tax saving is spread over a short period. A dollar of withholding tax saving has relatively greater return impact over the life of a short-term position than it does over the life of a longer-term position. For a more thorough understanding of this application, the reader should consult Chapter 5.

A SYNTHETIC LONG STOCK POSITION AS A CASH MANAGEMENT OVERLAY

To the extent that an investor can earn an enhanced fixed income return through superior credit analysis or duration management, an enhanced return on investible cash can make the synthetic position attractive relative to the actual stock position. A portfolio consisting of a variety of synthetic positions may give a manager a variety of intermediate and longer term opportunities to enhance fixed income returns. Investors with unusual fixed income portfolio management capabilities may find synthetic positions particularly attractive.[3]

The options literature is replete with examples of alternate ways to take risk equivalent positions using very different amounts of cash. From a risk perspective and assuming European-style exercise, a short put is the equivalent of a covered call. A long call is the risk equivalent of a long stock position plus a long put. Buying a call and selling a put at the same strike price creates a synthetic long stock position. Setting aside the differences between European and American exercise styles and some margin and credit issues, the major difference between these paired risk equivalent positions is the cash commitment that an investor must make. The covered call writer who

---

[3] A number of fixed income managers have created enhanced stock index products by combining S&P 500 stock index futures contracts with aggressively managed fixed income portfolios. See Karen Damato, "Pimco Fund Beats S&P 500 With Bonds," *Wall Street Journal* (December 5, 1996). Extending this technique to an actively managed synthetic stock portfolio is an obvious opportunity.

is long the stock and short a call is making a substantial cash commitment to a position which can have a relatively modest stock market exposure. The investor who takes a risk equivalent position by selling a put will deposit collateral as security and receive cash from the sale of the option. The fact that the sale of a put generates cash rather than absorbing it provides opportunities and requirements for cash management that are very different from the cash management position of the covered call writer. Figure 4 illustrates the risk comparability of alternate ways of taking various positions. The level of each solid or dashed line on the vertical axis indicates return differences that depend largely on the respective cash requirements of the alternatives. Figure 1 in Chapter 5 and the accompanying text illustrate the same point with a synthetic stock position established with options.

Any investor taking a short option position is required to post a performance bond in any of a variety of forms (an option guarantee letter, an escrow receipt, or direct deposit of collateral). Credit issues are rarely significant from the investor's perspective because the exchange-traded option counterparty, the Options Clearing Corporation, is rated AAA. Similarly, large equity portfolio managers rarely find it difficult to meet any reasonable margin or collateral requirement. Even the manager of a highly leveraged equity or equity-equivalent portfolio can usually arrange margin easily. Nonetheless, some investors may be intrigued by opportunities to make a lower margin deposit on some synthetic positions than a conventional long or short stock position would require.

Assuming there are no significant valuation discrepancies among the options involved, alternative equivalent positions can play a useful role in adjusting the composition of a portfolio to actual or expected cash flows. For some portfolios, the ability to take a sizable position with little cash can help anticipate cash flow, control leverage, or generate cash for an enhanced money-market return strategy. Index funds combining enhanced money market or longer maturity fixed income strategies with stock index futures have become almost commonplace.[4] The availability of Equity FLEX options lets active equity managers combine their stock selection skills with the skills of colleagues who run enhanced money market portfolios. Some features of these applications are developed at greater length in Chapter 5.

---

[4] Damato, "Pimco Fund Beats S&P 500 With Bonds."

Figure 4a: Profit/Loss Pattern of Covered Write versus Short Put

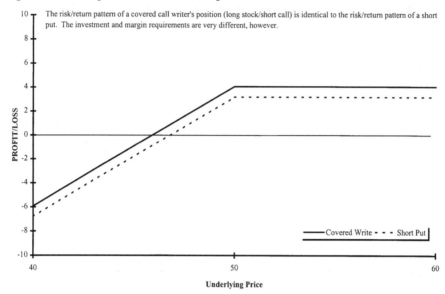

The risk/return pattern of a covered call writer's position (long stock/short call) is identical to the risk/return pattern of a short put. The investment and margin requirements are very different, however.

Figure 4b: Profit/Loss Pattern of Short Straddle versus Short Neutral Option Hedge (Long Stock, Short Two Calls)

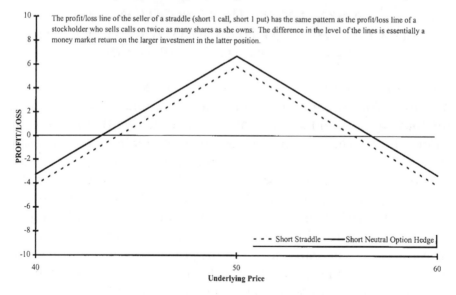

The profit/loss line of the seller of a straddle (short 1 call, short 1 put) has the same pattern as the profit/loss line of a stockholder who sells calls on twice as many shares as she owns. The difference in the level of the lines is essentially a money market return on the larger investment in the latter position.

Figure 4c: Profit/Loss Pattern of Long Straddle versus Long Neutral Option Hedge* (Short Stock, Long Two Calls)

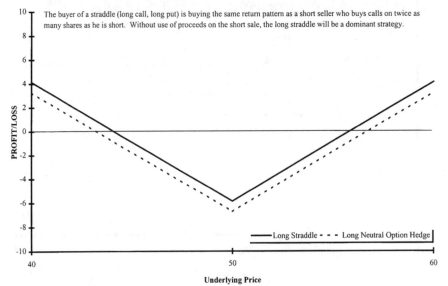

The buyer of a straddle (long call, long put) is buying the same return pattern as a short seller who buys calls on twice as many shares as he is short. Without use of proceeds on the short sale, the long straddle will be a dominant strategy.

* Assumes no use of proceeds on short sale.

A SYNTHETIC SHORT POSITION — REDUCING THE COST OF BORROWING STOCK AND PROTECTING AGAINST BUY-INS

Equity FLEX options can be used to create synthetic short stock positions. An investor who is only an occasional short seller may find buying puts and selling calls more attractive that an outright short sale. A synthetic short stock position created with European style Equity FLEX options offers complete protection against a buy-in if the underlying stock becomes hard to borrow. While the value of this buy-in protection may be reflected in the option premiums, avoiding the risk of having to cover the short prematurely may be worth any additional cost of using options — particularly if the investor is not generally active in the stock loan market. Investors who are active and experienced short-sellers may find it profitable to sell the actual short position and buy the synthetic long position — the other side of the option structure necessary to create the synthetic short position in options. These experienced investors are, in effect, selling "buy-in insurance" to a less comfortable short seller. This application is discussed in more detail in Chapter 5.

IMPLEMENTING A VOLATILITY VIEWPOINT — PROFITING FROM A LARGER FRACTION OF AN INSTITUTION'S INVESTMENT RESEARCH

Most institutional investors use only a small fraction of the information that they acquire through their in-house research efforts and from street research. The integration of Equity FLEX options into the portfolio management process makes more of this information useful to an investment manager. Most stock or company research focuses on the outlook for corporate earnings reports and on specific corporate and product developments. The emphasis is on the likely *direction* of stock price movement. Relatively few analysts and portfolio managers stress the historic and prospective volatility — the *magnitude* of common stock price movements — and the impact of earnings reports and other events on volatility. One reason for this emphasis is that it has not been easy for large investors to profit from being right on volatility. If investors can profit from informed judgments on likely future volatility, they are using more of the research information they have developed. They can add value by virtue of the fact that there is far less competition in volatility estimation than in earnings estimation. If research provides a detailed expectation of a volatility pattern or of limitations on price behavior, options can be useful in structuring a payout pattern tailored to the expectation.

The diagram in Figure 5 illustrates one example of a structured payout. In this specific example, the investor has concluded that the most likely price for the stock at the time the component options expire is close to the peak in the pattern illustrated. The investor also believes that the chance of a large stock price decline is limited and, if there is any volatility risk, it is on the upside. These expectations suggest a payout structure that provides neutral results if the stock price runs away on the upside. Obviously, this pattern is only illustrative.

Figure 5: A Structured Payout with Options

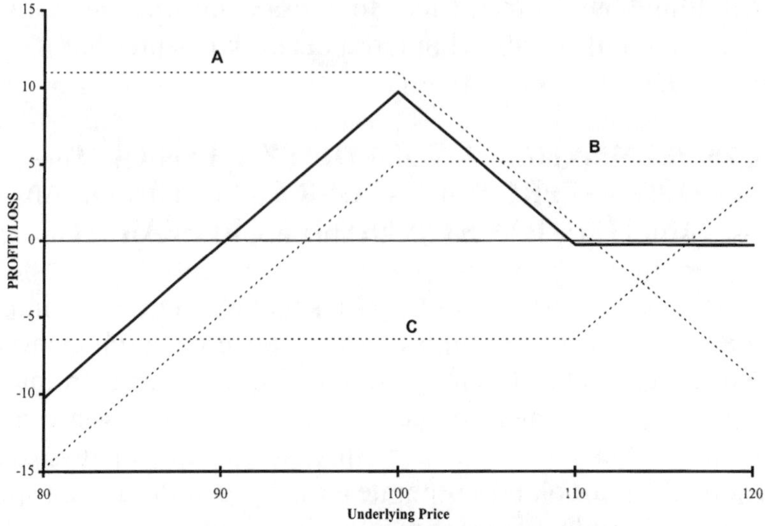

	Strike	Maturity	Line
Sell 1 Put	100	1 year	A
Sell 1 Call	100	1 year	B
Buy 1 Call	110	1 year	C

Most institutional investors will use options primarily to reflect general volatility views rather than highly specific expectations for price patterns, but many possibilities are available. Opportunities include the simple sale of a call on a stock that an investor expects to be less volatile in the near term than its option premium implies or purchase of a put to provide downside protection on a position which the manager feels has excellent long term prospects and significant near term risk — with the risk not fully reflected in the pricing of the options.

TEMPORARY MARKET EXPOSURE REDUCTION AND TAX DEFERRAL

Several option techniques can be used to maintain a position in an underlying stock during a period when the investor wishes to reduce exposure to that stock's price movement. Selling calls and buying puts are the traditional option transactions used to reduce exposure to an underlying stock held in a portfolio. Occasionally these trans-

actions are combined to create a collar or "risk reversal" as illustrated in Figure 6. Equity FLEX options are easy to use to create a
zero-premium collar, a market risk control structure that has been
popular in the OTC options market.

Collars and other options positions may be used to defer taxes
and delay the recognition of gains for other purposes. For taxable
accounts, a degree of care must be exercised in taking risk offsetting
options positions because the tax treatment of these positions can be
tricky. Certain option positions will interrupt an investor's holding
period if the position is not yet long term, acting as the equivalent of a
short sale. Other option positions have no effect on holding period or
cost basis. Consultation with professional tax counsel is always a
good idea if a position has significant tax exposure. Investors should
be alert to challenges to these and other techniques designed to defer
realization of gains. Forthcoming Internal Revenue Service Regulations under the Taxpayer Relief Act of 1997 will almost certainly
constrain the use of options to reduce stock market risk and defer
taxes. Risk management opportunities will not be eliminated, but they
will inevitably become more complex. For a brief discussion of tax
considerations affecting some offsetting positions, see Appendix B.

Figure 6: Zero Cost Collar

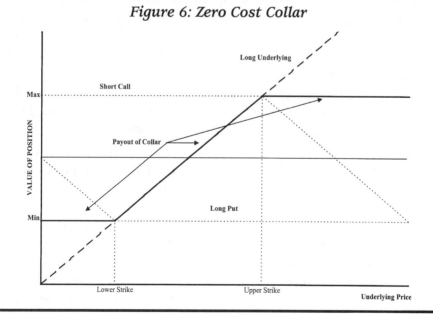

REDUCING COUNTERPARTY RISK AND
CAPITAL REQUIREMENTS

To reduce counterparty risk, broker/dealers may wish to consider using Equity FLEX options to facilitate a customer transaction instead of entering into an OTC contract. Since the AAA-rated Options Clearing Corporation is the counter party to every Equity FLEX trade, the customer and the broker/dealer do not have to worry that the credit risk of the counterparty is too high. In some instances, a broker/dealer may find Equity FLEX options to be an appealing alternative to the establishment of the kind of highly-capitalized AAA-rated subsidiary which some firms have created specifically for the purpose of engaging in OTC derivatives transactions. Serendipitously, some firms may find that executing the trade on an exchange floor results in lower capital requirements for maintaining any ongoing position related to the trade.

Dealers specializing in OTC transactions will develop a wide range of Equity FLEX substitution and risk management applications. Some of these will be cost motivated and some will use the Equity FLEX price discovery process to ensure price transparency.

ISOLATING RISKS FOR ACCEPTANCE OR AVOIDANCE

Exchange-traded options are used frequently by risk arbitrageurs as a way to divide and reallocate the risk of a position and to permit the risk arbitrageur to accept certain risks and avoid others. Comparison of option premiums on contracts with expiration dates before and after expiration of a tender offer, a shareholder vote, or a board meeting are common methods of measuring the market's expectation for the outcome of these events. With Equity FLEX options, investors or arbitrageurs with somewhat different perspectives on an event or corporate development can allocate the risk among themselves in a way that reflects each entity's expectations, risk preferences, and valuation estimates. The limitations on expiration dates with standardized options and the credit issues which often cloud OTC option contract discussions can be eliminated, and relatively "pure" risks can be taken and avoided with Equity FLEX contracts.

The use of options to isolate risks is such a broad topic that no single example can be comprehensively typical. Nonetheless, suppose, for example, that the monthly expiration date for standard options is July 17 and a corporate earnings report is due on July 21. The period leading up to an earnings report, particularly an uncertain earnings report is usually a period of higher stock price volatility than a randomly selected period of equal length. The relative pricing of at-, in-, and out-of-the-money puts and calls for July and August expiration will reflect something close to consensus expectation for the impact of the earnings report on stock price levels and volatility. The August options will often discount a higher expected volatility than would be appropriate for the entire period between the July and August expirations. Although transaction costs may limit the chance to profit, an astute analyst may be able to take in enough premium from an option expiring just after the earnings report to drastically reduce the cost of a long August option. The opportunity to adjust the strike price of an Equity FLEX put and, soon, an Equity FLEX call, may offer option combinations that let the astute analyst surrender payout segments he considers of low value and acquire payout segments he values highly. The opportunity to apply both statistical and intuitive analyses of earnings reports, management changes, merger workouts, and any other uncertain corporate development to the purchase and sale of Equity FLEX and standard option combinations is an intriguing possibility with unlimited applications.

RENEWING CORPORATE CAPITAL LOSSES

In the United States, a corporation cannot deduct capital losses against ordinary income; but it can carry capital losses forward against the day when it generates capital gains. Corporate capital loss carry forwards are generally limited to five years, but regulated investment companies can carry losses forward for eight years. Corporations can carry foreign expropriation capital losses forward ten years. While the straddle rules limit opportunities to defer gains, there seems to be no objection to realizing a gain to use an expiring capital loss carry forward and deferring an offsetting loss to the next tax year. The new loss starts the capital loss aging process anew. Here, as indicated in an earlier context, consultation with a tax advisor is appropriate.

BUYING PUTS AS DEFAULT INSURANCE

Another intriguing Equity FLEX application is the purchase of puts by the corporation or by one of its creditors as protection against default. There are obvious conflicts if the corporation buys puts on its own stock because management has a great deal of control over the subsequent value of the puts. A creditor, on the other hand, can use any profit on a put to offset default losses without an obvious influence on either the default or the value of the put. This application, described in a recent article, illustrates the range of possibilities that will develop.[5]

The portfolio applications we have listed and described are the result of a preliminary attempt to codify some of the more obvious portfolio uses of Equity FLEX options. Many of these suggestions are simple extensions of widely used techniques; others, such as the block trading implementations, are only possible with one or more of the features of Equity FLEX. Innovative portfolio managers will want to read the chapter on synthetic stock as a possible source of other applications.

---

[5] See Austin Murphy, "Buying Put Options to Insure Against Bankruptcy," *The Journal of Financial Engineering* (December 1997), pp. 307-319.

Chapter 4

Equity FLEX Options and Corporate Stock Repurchase Programs

S elling put options as part of a corporate stock repurchase program is not a new or unusual practice. Conversations with long-time option traders reveal that some corporate financial officers sold puts as part of their stock repurchase programs long before the Securities and Exchange Commission issued a no-action letter assenting to the sale of exchange-traded puts in corporate stock repurchase programs.[1] Although media discussions of corporate treasury put sales mention fewer than a dozen companies by name, the consensus of option-trading desks is that at least 10% of the public companies that repurchase their stock on the open market now use put sales as part of the repurchase program.[2]

A put sold by the issuer of the option's underlying common stock gives the put holder the right to sell the stock to the corporation. If the stock is below the strike price of the put at expiration, the option will be exercised and the corporation will buy its stock back. But because the holder is not obliged to sell the stock to the corporation if the stock is selling above the strike price, selling puts is not a perfect substitute for outright repurchase of the stock. Figure 3 in the previous chapter compares the payoff pattern associated with buying back the stock outright to the payoff pattern from selling the put.

---

[1] SEC File No. TP 90-375.

[2] A number of articles describing put sales in stock repurchase programs have appeared in business periodicals. See, for example, Philip L. Zweig, "Stock Buybacks Are Back — With a Twist," *Business Week* (August 29, 1994), p.70; Nick Gilbert, "House Odds: Intel Has Made Millions From Derivatives — So Far," *Financial World* (May 23, 1995), pp. 22-24; Lawrence Richter Quinn, "Can Corporates Really Use Equity Derivatives?" *Derivatives Strategy* (February 20, 1994), pp. 20-24; and Thomas N. Cochran, "The Striking Price," *Barrons* (February 6, 1995). The small number of companies mentioned by name seems to reflect dealers' natural desire to avoid inviting competitors to call their clients.

If we assume that the put strike is equal to the price of the stock when the put is sold and that the choice is between selling the put and buying the stock outright at the time the put is sold, the tradeoffs are clear. Suppose that Random Corporation wishes to repurchase some of its stock, which is now selling for $50. It sells a put option for $2 per share. Simplifying slightly,

- If the stock price at expiration is below the strike, the corporation is better off selling the put versus outright stock purchase by the amount of the option premium. If the stock price at expiration is $40, the put is still exercised at $50. Random thus buys back the stock at a net price of $48, $2 better than the $50 at which it would have otherwise bought the stock.
- If the stock price at expiration is above the put strike but below the strike plus the initial option premium the corporation is better off selling the put by some part of the option premium. If the stock price at expiration is $51, the option is not exercised. Random buys back the stock at $51. With the $2 proceeds of the option, the net cost to Random is $49, $1 less than it would have otherwise paid to buy the stock at $50 instead of selling the put.
- If the stock is above the put strike plus the option premium at expiration, the corporation has an opportunity cost relative to buying stock outright instead of using the put. If the stock price at expiration is $55, the option is not exercised. Random buys back the stock at $55. With the $2 proceed of the option, the stock cost Random $3 more than it would have otherwise paid.

So far, the use of puts, although not equivalent to an outright stock purchase, may seem straightforward. But choosing between the alternatives is complicated by cash flow timing issues, volatility and valuation analysis, and SEC regulations covering stock repurchase. One purpose of this chapter is to review some of the issues determining how a corporation deals with stock repurchase — with or without the sale of puts.

The SEC's no-action letter on the use of puts in stock repurchase (cited above) referred only to exchange-traded puts. However, most corporations and their attorneys and investment bankers have interpreted the SEC's position as equally accommodating to over-the-counter (OTC) put options. The greater flexibility of OTC options terms — before Equity FLEX — led to heavy use of OTC puts in stock repurchase programs. The introduction of exchange-traded Equity FLEX puts on the American Stock Exchange and several other exchanges should change this pattern and bring many stock repurchase-linked put trades to the Exchange floor.

SOME REASONS FOR CORPORATE STOCK REPURCHASE

Corporate "distributions" of cash to shareholders through stock repurchase are not yet as large as dividend payments, but the value of stock repurchased has grown much more rapidly than dividend distributions since the early 1980s. U.S. companies bought back $176 billion of their own stock in 1996, a 78% increase over repurchases in 1995, the previous record year.[3] Some equity analysts have even begun to stress the need to consider the record level of stock repurchases before lamenting low dividend payments or inferring increased market risk from low dividend yields.[4]

A comprehensive review of the reasons behind corporate stock repurchase programs is outside the scope of this volume, but it does seem appropriate to review some of the arguments advanced for stock repurchase as an alternative to increased dividends, aggressive capital expenditure programs, retirement of debt, or other ways of "disposing" of high levels of corporate cash.[5]

- Corporate stock repurchase is more tax efficient for the typical shareholder than an increase in the company's cash dividend.

---

[3] Erin Davies, "What's Right About Corporate Cash Flow," *Fortune* (March 31, 1997), p. 28.

[4] Daniel Kadlec, "The Unyielding Market," *Time* (December 2, 1996), p. 57. For a slightly different perspective, see Kevin Cole, Jean Helwege, and David Laster, "Stock Market Valuation Indicators: Is This Time Different?" *Financial Analysts Journal* (May/June 1996), pp. 56-64.

[5] An excellent discussion of the cost of capital and capitalization structure issues can be found in Dennis Soter, Eugene Brigham, and Paul Evanson, "The Dividend Cut Heard 'Round the World: The Case of FPL," *Journal of Applied Corporate Finance* (Spring 1996), pp. 4-15.

Specifically, investors who need more cash can sell shares at a demand-enhanced price. Shareholders who do not need cash are not forced to pay taxes on a dividend distribution. Furthermore, tax rates on capital gains are lower than tax rates on dividends for most taxpayers.[6]

- Corporate stock repurchase programs ensure that there will be some demand for stock at times when ordinary investment demand might be limited. This suggests, on balance, a higher stock price — if for no other reason than the dynamic interaction of demand and supply. Concentration of ownership of the firm over fewer shares could play an important role in the longer-term valuation of the stock.

- Corporate stock repurchase programs can be used to "signal" management's positive outlook to shareholders and to the market. A stock repurchase program is usually an indication that management is relatively bullish on the stock and, more specifically, that investment in stock repurchase competes favorably with other investment opportunities, including acquisitions and internal capital investments.[7]

- Corporate stock repurchase programs can reassure the market that management will not make unwise internal investments or cash acquisitions just to create a larger corporation.

- Although shareholders may be ambivalent on this point, a stock repurchase program may help a corporation avoid a takeover attempt stimulated by a low stock price. A low stock price may attract an initial bid, but shareholders may be better

---

[6] Suppose that Successful Co. has 100 shares outstanding worth $10 each, representing net assets with a market value of $1,000 including $100 of excess cash. If the firm pays out the $100 as dividends, all the shareholders pay taxes at their normal marginal tax rate, which we will assume to be 39.6%. The shareholders thus get to keep $60.40 of the dividends. If the firm instead repurchases $100 worth of stock, only the selling shareholders will pay any taxes at all, and they probably will be taxed at the long-term capital gains rate of 20%. Even if the selling shareholders have a zero basis in the stock, they will get to keep $80.00 after taxes. Shareholders who do not want to sell will own a larger fraction of the firm and they do not have to pay any immediate tax — their taxes are deferred until they finally sell in the future. Clearly, stock repurchases are much more tax-efficient than dividends in transferring excess cash from the firm to its shareholders.

[7] IBM's announcement of an up to $3.5 billion stock repurchase plan was — rightly or wrongly — widely cited as contributing to the market's quick recovery in October 1997.

off if any takeover bidding starts at a higher stock price level. On the other hand, a large stock repurchase program may make pooling-of-interests accounting in a merger impossible, thus frustrating some business combinations.

- A stock repurchase program is often an efficient way to acquire shares for dividend reinvestment plans (DRIPs) and employee benefit programs based on stock purchase by employees (including employee stock options).

This list of reasons for corporate stock repurchase is not exhaustive and arguments on the other side of the question are occasionally offered. For some firms, the funds used for the stock buyback might be invested more productively within the firm. Also, if a firm repurchases too many shares, the liquidity of the remaining shares could suffer. On balance, many corporations have concluded that stock repurchase should be an important part of their earnings per share enhancement, cash management, employee benefits, and shareholder relations programs. On average, 600 open-market stock repurchase programs were announced by U.S. corporations each year between 1990 and 1995.[8]

SELLING PUTS VERSUS OPEN MARKET STOCK REPURCHASE

Once the decision to repurchase stock has been made, the corporate financial staff's attention naturally turns to the optimal repurchase technique, with significant attention focused on the sale of put options as an alternative to outright purchase of shares. Given the plethora of rules covering corporate stock repurchase programs, the case for using puts as part of the repurchase plan is surprisingly simple. We assume, as do most corporate financial officers managing repurchase programs, that the underlying common stock is cheap. This does not suggest that aggressive repurchase is always better than careful accumulation of the underlying stock, but it does suggest that the perceived cheapness of the stock is a reason to encourage the corporation to take advantage of opportunities to maximize stock repurchase.

---

[8] David L. Ikenberry and Theo Vermaelen, "The Option to Repurchase Stock," *Financial Management* (Winter 1996), pp. 9-24.

One specific rationale for the use of puts in a repurchase program is that there may be an opportunity to sell puts for more than their fair value. An option analyst will relate option value to the volatility of the underlying stock. If the put premium discounts a higher level of volatility than management deems likely over the life of the put contract, then the put is overpriced on a valuation basis. The corporation should profit on balance by selling the put. The trade-off between the put premium received and the opportunity cost of not buying the stock outright (illustrated in Figure 3 of the previous chapter) is the essence of the relationship between stock price volatility and option valuation. Of course, the decision to sell a put does not irretrievably commit the issuer to an unlimited opportunity loss in a rising market. Subject to volume limitations, the issuer can step in and repurchase the put and buy the stock outright if the stock begins to rise. Correspondingly, the issuer can repurchase puts if the stock begins a share price decline.

In some respects, a more controversial valuation issue than valuation of the options is the strength and accuracy of management's conviction that its shares are undervalued. To the extent that management turns out to be right, selling a put leads to collection of an option premium in exchange for the contingent right to sell stock to the corporation at a price that is below the corporation's forecast of the stock's expected value. While the notion that corporate financial officers enjoy above-average ability to predict the behavior of their own firm's stock is controversial, this reasoning does enter into a number of put sale decisions.[9]

---

[9] The title of a recent article epitomizes the issue: Jacob M. Schlessinger, "CEOs Say Stocks, Except Their Own, Are Too High," *Wall Street Journal* (February 27, 1997). One study by Eli Bartov, Itzak Krinsky, and Jason Lee, "Evidence on How Companies Choose Between Dividends and Open-Market Stock Repurchases," *Journal of Applied Corporate Finance* (Spring 1998), pp. 89-96, finds evidence that stock repurchase as a dividend substitute is linked to stock undervaluation, extensive use of management stock options, and heavy institutional stock ownership. Not incidentally, the quality of management's market forecasts may not be reflected in earnings reports. Transactions in puts, like transactions in the company's stock itself, flow through the equity account without a first-order effect on earnings. Effective with the publication of the Financial Accounting Standards Board's Statement of Financial Accounting Standards no. 128, in-the-money written put options may affect the calculation of diluted earnings per share. FASB now requires a diluted earnings per share calculation based on the reverse treasury stock method. See paragraph 24 and footnote 14 of SFAS no. 128.

Selling put options can also add flexibility to the timing of stock repurchases. SEC Rule 10b-18 limits stock purchases by the issuer to 25% of the average daily trading volume of its stock. Selling a put counts against the daily stock volume on the day the put is sold, not on the day it is exercised. If stock volume is high during a period that precedes the availability of cash flow to finance share purchases, it may be advantageous to sell some puts to take full advantage of the high volume, with the expectation that cash will be available when the puts mature. In this case, the put is a kind of deferred purchase contract that is designed to match opportunity (i.e., high stock volume) with later cash flow. A related reason for the use of put sales linked to cash flow expectations is that selling puts when put values are high may leave scope for even more stock repurchases if cash flow increases beyond expectations.

EXCHANGE-TRADED EQUITY FLEX VERSUS OTC PUTS

The shortcomings of standardized exchange-traded options that led to growth in OTC put transactions have been eliminated in the Equity FLEX environment. Specifically, option contract position limits do not apply to Equity FLEX options. Also, Equity FLEX puts offer the ability to select any strike price or exercise date (except the expiration date of a standard option and two business days before and after that date) and the ability to select either European or American exercise style.[10]

While the disadvantages formerly associated with exchange-traded options are gone, the advantages remain. Access to the Exchange brings enhanced liquidity and more transparent pricing. Open price discovery is probably the most important advantage of the exchange environment. Should the corporate seller of a put in a stock repurchase program wish to repurchase the put before it is exercised, the corporation is no longer linked exclusively to a single OTC option dealer. An Equity FLEX transaction is, in some ways, as much a bilateral transaction as a direct contract with an OTC dealer;

---

[10] A European-style option can be exercised only on its expiration date. An American-style option can be exercised on any business day prior to and including the expiration day.

but the fact that the Options Clearing Corporation serves as intermediary gives other dealers the opportunity and the incentive to step in to ensure a fair price on any repurchase of the puts. The dissemination of the Equity FLEX "request for quote" to a wide range of dealers (on and off the floor) ensures more efficient price discovery than telephone calls to a few OTC dealers possibly can.[11] As summarized here and in Table 1, the historic reasons for favoring OTC puts have been eliminated by the introduction of Equity FLEX put options.

Table 1: Comparison of OTC and Equity-Flex Puts Sold by Stock's Issuer in Stock Repurchase Program

	OTC	Exchange-Traded Equity-FLEX
Subject to stock volume linked stock repurchase limitations	Yes	Yes
Absence of option position limits	Yes[*]	Yes
Full range of available strikes	Yes	Yes
Choice of American or European exercise	Yes	Yes
Buyers	Usually a single dealer who may hedge on the Exchange or resell the OTC option	Bids are solicited on the Exchange floor and from dealers and investors off the floor
Seller collateral requirement	Negotiable	Usually a standard margin or collateral deposit or an option guarantee letter issued by a bank

* Position limits do not apply to the cash-settled put common in the OTC market if the dealer is a domestic or foreign bank or insurance company. Certain securities dealers may be subject to position limits on cash-settled stock options. Presumably, physically-settled OTC options will qualify for the Equity FLEX exemption from position limits if they conform to the exercise date restrictions applied to Equity FLEX options.

---

[11] These features and other advantages of exchange traded options were highlighted in a speech by SEC chairman, Arthur Levitt, "The Options Markets: A Cornerstone of U.S. Capital Markets Today," delivered at the 13th Annual Risk Management Conference, Tucson, Arizona, January 30, 1997.

Chapter 5

The Economics of Synthetic Stock Based on Equity FLEX Options

In this chapter we offer an extended discussion of synthetic long and short stock equivalent positions taken with Equity FLEX options for several reasons. First, this discussion integrates options with underlying markets in a way that may be useful or enlightening to some readers. Second, it may spark ideas for new applications because it is more generalized than the earlier application discussion. Finally, it begins to quantify some of the costs and opportunities applicable to Equity FLEX markets.

PUT-CALL PARITY AND SYNTHETIC STOCK

Creating a synthetic stock position with options relies on the simple European put-call parity equation found in introductory options texts. For a European put, P, and call, C, with the same maturity, T, and the same exercise price, E, on a stock with price, S, that pays dividends over the life of the option with present value, D, put-call parity can be expressed:

$$S + P = Ee^{-rT} + C + D \qquad (1)$$

Rearranging the terms of the parity equation to stress stock equivalence, we obtain:

$$S = C - P + Ee^{-rT} + D \qquad (2)$$

In words, equation (2) states that *at fair values for all the instruments*, a stock provides exactly the same payoff as buying a call, selling a put, and investing the present value of the exercise price and the dividends at the risk free rate, r. Figure 1 illustrates the payout structure of a synthetic stock position and its components and compares the resulting payouts with an actual stock position.

Figure 1: Synthetic versus
Actual Long Stock Position Payoff Diagrams
A. Synthetic

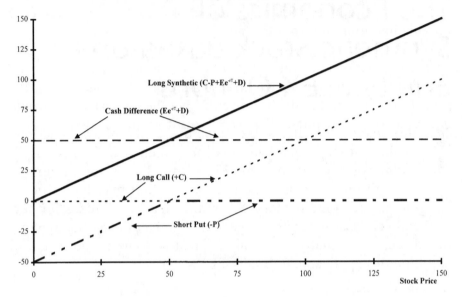

B. Actual

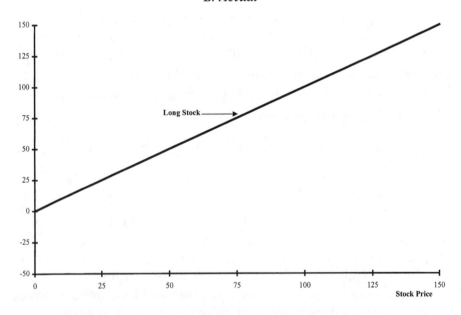

The obvious question is why anyone would go to the trouble of putting together a synthetic stock position when they can just buy the real thing. The answer to this disingenuous question is that a synthetic position can soften the impact of regulatory constraints or provide important return or tax advantages.

An interesting historic use of put-call parity was to create synthetic positions to avoid usury laws which placed restrictions on interest rates. The lender would buy a stock and a put, and at the same time sell a call to the borrower. Either the put or the call would be exercised, and put-call parity would insure that the lender received a fixed payoff from the borrower. The interest rate was never explicitly stated in the contract, but it was built into the difference between the original cost of the position to the lender and the amount received at maturity (exercise). Russell Sage, the 19th century financier, was famous for using this technique.[1]

Today, there is little need to use put-call parity to avoid usury restrictions; but contemporary regulatory work-arounds may include sidestepping restrictions on cross border stock holdings, avoiding restrictions on stock transferability, or tax deferral. While the flexibility of synthetic stock is appropriately interesting, our immediate focus is on the comparative economics of actual and synthetic stock. All applications will turn, at least in part, on these economics.

As indicated in Chapter 3, the economic advantages of synthetic stock are very specific and, in a well-defined application, they should be readily measurable. For example, a tax exempt U.S.-based investor with a comparative advantage in managing cash may find a synthetic stock position superior to owning the stock itself because the opportunity to earn a higher return by managing the cash separately has significant value. A synthetic stock position may also help a cross-border investor in U.S. stocks to reduce the tax impact of U.S. dividend withholding taxes. On the other side of a transaction, an investor who wishes to hold a short position in a stock may find a synthetic short (buying a put and selling a call) preferable to a standard short position which may require payment of an explicit or implicit fee for stock borrowing.

---

[1] Synthetic payoffs to avoid usury restrictions go back literally thousands of years. See Michael S. Knoll, "Put Call Parity and the Law," Working Paper 94-12, USC Law School.

The purpose of this chapter is to compare the economics of the Equity FLEX option version of synthetic stock with the economics of the more traditional way of taking actual long and short common stock positions. Our conclusion is that the synthetic can offer a significantly enhanced return to both buyers and sellers.

A synthetic stock transaction should be evaluated relative to the best alternative way of taking the equivalent long or short stock position. The best alternative in a particular instance may be an equity swap or a position in a deep in-the-money put or call — possibilities beyond the scope of the present analysis. In other cases, *the best choice may depend on the nature and nationality of the nominal and beneficial holders of the position, tax exposures, regulatory constraints, and, to a lesser extent, institutional structure.* While we discuss some of these issues, we have not attempted to quantify their impact beyond measurable economic differences between Equity FLEX synthetic stock and standard long or short stock positions.

The first step in comparing synthetic stock to actual stock positions for both long investors and short sellers is to make a direct comparison between the investment-adjusted returns for the synthetic long position and the more traditional stock alternative. We look first at the pretax or untaxed long positions and then at the special circumstances which may affect the relative attractiveness of actual and synthetic long positions for certain investors. We make a similar comparison for actual and synthetic short positions. We come away not with an unequivocal endorsement of the synthetic or actual long or short, but rather with a process that a portfolio manager can use to determine the economics applicable to a particular portfolio.

LONG STOCK VERSUS LONG SYNTHETIC — THE ROLE OF THE IMPLIED REPO RATE

A long stock position combines a return from the investment of cash with a return based on fluctuations in the value of the underlying equity. The synthetic position, to oversimplify only slightly, separates the cash and equity returns. An investor with an advantage in cash management may enhance a portfolio's overall return with synthetics because he can invest the cash at a higher return than the rate imbedded in the actual stock position. The synthetic, through the long call and short put, provides direct exposure to changes in the price of the underlying stock. The initial pricing of the synthetic's European-style component options incorporates the impact of expected dividends. The cash return from the synthetic will be earned on a separate investment in money market or other fixed income instruments — or, in a few cases, from interest saved by a reduction in borrowing. The investor will compare the total cash flows available from the long call, short put, and money market/fixed income investment to the cash flows on the actual stock. Figure 1 illustrates, in an approximate way, the separation of cash and equity return components.

Synthetic stock positions are not yet a common phenomenon in the Equity FLEX market. Consequently, it is too early to tell if there will be a standard pattern for quoting, evaluating, or comparing actual and synthetic stock positions. However, standards associated with similar positions and transactions — stock index products in particular — can be useful in evaluating synthetic stock.

The broker or dealer offering a synthetic position will calculate an implied repo rate (IRR) or, as it is sometimes called, a return to the hedged portfolio (RHP). Whatever the name, this rate is simply the rate that must be earned on the time-weighted cash difference between the money committed to the long stock position and the money committed to the synthetic position to make the positions fully equivalent. A posted implied repo rate may or may not reflect the position of a specific investor, so any assumptions behind the calculation should be evaluated carefully. An appropriate implied repo rate calculation will incorporate realistic assumptions on the amount and timing of any cash dividends expected on the stock and foregone on the synthetic, and it should cover the exact period until the expiration of the options. Lastly, it is important to note that the implied repo rate calculation may or may not incorporate the cost of liquidating the position.[2]

---

[2] Unless there is a specific charge associated with option exercise, the relevant cost of liquidating the position should be essentially the same in each case: one stock commission on a market-on-close order. If the actual stock is held, the investor will simply sell it with a market-on-close order on the expiration day. If the synthetic is held, the investor will be exercising a call and selling stock with a market-on-close order or buying stock with a market-on-close order and delivering the stock against exercise of the put.

To illustrate an implied repo calculation, assume an investor is considering taking a synthetic position in Philip Morris (MO), with the stock offered at $45 and expected quarterly dividends of $0.40 per share. The 6-month at-the-money call is 6 bid and the 6-month at-the-money put is offered at 5½ for a net synthetic short position credit equal to the difference between the two — $0.50 in this case. Assuming the investor will buy the stock for cash, as opposed to buying on margin, the cash flows associated with buying and holding the stock for six months are an initial outlay of $45 and income of $0.40 at the end of three and six months. For the synthetic position, the initial credit is $0.50.

A margin deposit will be required on the short call position; however, any position taken will be part of a portfolio, so the margin requirements are easily covered for most equity investors. The IRR or RHP (r) for this example turns out to be just under 6%. The actual rate may vary if dividends paid during the period are different from levels assumed. The underlying math with S equal to the stock price and r equal to the implied repo-rate is:

Cash Flows:	T_0	T_1	T_2
Long Stock	−$45	+$0.40	+$0.40 +$S_2$
Short Synthetic	+$0.50		+$45 −$S_2$
Net Cash Flow	−$44.50	+$0.40	+$45.40

So:

$$0 = -44.50 + 0.40\frac{1}{(1+r)^{\frac{1}{4}}} + 45.40\frac{1}{(1+r)^{\frac{1}{2}}}$$

$$\Rightarrow r = 5.955\%$$

Since the other side of the transaction occurs at the same prices, the IRR on the long and the short synthetic differ by the effect of any commission on the trade. If the investor initiating the synthetic pays a spread, it may be useful to calculate separate rates for synthetics initiated by the buyer and the seller of the synthetic.

In the simplest case, an untaxed domestic investor can compare the pretax implied repo rate with the rate she expects to earn on a money market instrument that matures (or is sold) on the option expiration date. The implied repo rate may differ from a money market rate because the party on the other side of the trade may have a better opportunity, or may face a penalty in creating the synthetic. If an investor chooses to liquidate the position sooner or hold it longer than the date implied by the option expiration, an appropriate implied repo rate adjustment will be necessary. Ordinarily, the need for flexibility will make the actual stock position more attractive and the synthetic slightly less attractive than a simple comparison between the implied repo rate and the rate an investor can earn in the money market would suggest, but the difference should be small.[3]

To the extent that an investor can earn an enhanced fixed income return through superior credit analysis or duration management, an enhanced return on investible cash can make the synthetic position attractive relative to the actual stock position. A portfolio consisting of a variety of synthetic positions may give the manager a variety of intermediate and longer term opportunities to enhance fixed income returns. Investors with unusual fixed income portfolio management capabilities may find synthetic positions particularly attractive.[4] We will return to the economics of enhanced money market portfolios later in the chapter. First, however, we conclude our examination of actual versus synthetic returns on a long position with an example in which differential taxation of an actual stock position and the components of a synthetic produces different returns.

DIFFERENTIAL TAXATION OF DIVIDENDS AND INTEREST

To some cross-border investors an important feature of synthetic long stock positions is the opportunity to avoid the negative impact of the dividend withholding tax. Non-resident investors, whether their accounts are taxable or not in their home country, almost invariably pay a non-recoverable withholding tax on dividends they receive from U.S. stocks.[5] If the investor is resident in a tax treaty country,

---

[3] The major reason the difference should be small is that the charge to roll the position over will be an administrative or service charge, not a market impact charge.

[4] See Chapter 3, footnote 3.

the net withholding tax rate after a partial recovery is typically 15%. If the investor resides in a non-treaty country, the rate is 30%. A 2% yield to an investor in a 15% (treaty) country will generate a 30 basis point annual withholding tax. Table 1 in Chapter 3 shows the potential annual savings that foreign investors may receive by avoiding the U.S. withholding tax with a synthetic long stock position.

The appropriate dividend withholding calculation in a specific case is based on the period the options are outstanding. If the option has a life of thirty days and there is no dividend paid during that period, then no credit for saving a dividend withholding tax is attributable to the synthetic stock position. If, on the other hand, a thirty day option covers an ex-dividend date, the value of the withholding tax saving is spread over a short period. A dollar of withholding tax saving has relatively greater return impact over the life of a short-term option than it does over the life of a long-term option. The withholding tax saving requires a simple adjustment to the implied repo rate calculation and can be incorporated into that rate to compare the actual stock position to the synthetic for a foreign investor.

In contrast to the non-U.S. investor who stands to benefit from the synthetic position, a portfolio owned by a corporate taxpayer might benefit from the intercorporate dividend exclusion if it receives actual dividends. This adjustment can be incorporated in the implied repo rate comparison, but the likely impact of the intercorporate dividend exclusion is smaller than the withholding tax effect, and corporate portfolio stockholdings are minor. We do not expect this tax provision to lead to synthetic stock creation because the corporate stockholder will lose the dividend tax benefit if it sells a synthetic to hedge the market risk of an actual dividend-paying stock position.

ACTUAL VERSUS SYNTHETIC SHORTS — THE SHORT REBATE

While economic analysis of the short synthetic stock position has several similarities to the analysis of the long synthetic position, it

---

[5] The reason for the qualifying "almost" is that foreign government funds and a very few other foreign portfolios are exempt from the U.S. dividend withholding tax.

has some unique characteristics as well. Many investors who are frequent or consistent short sellers have arrangements with the brokerage firm carrying the short account to receive an interest-like payment called a *short rebate*. The short rebate is a payment in lieu of part of the interest that an investor selling stock short would receive on the proceeds of the short sale if that investor actually received the proceeds and could invest them at interest. Short sale proceeds can be invested at interest by whatever entity holds them until the short position is covered, but the proceeds are almost invariably held and invested by the securities lender, not by the short seller.

A complicating factor in calculating the value of short sale proceeds is that the broker must borrow stock to deliver on the sale and, like the short seller, both the broker and the lender of the stock also expect to share in the interest on the proceeds in the form of a fee or some other compensation for handling the stock loan. The short rebate, therefore, will be less than a money market rate by an amount reflecting (1) the cost of borrowing the stock from an investor or broker who holds it and (2) an administrative charge by the broker who carries the short position and arranges the stock loan.

There is limited standardization in the way short rebates are quoted. Some firms base their rebate rates on commercial paper or T-bill rates, but a common benchmark rate for short rebates is the fed funds rate, an overnight rate which reflects the brief and often unpredictable term of many short stock positions. The appropriateness of the fed funds rate as a measure of what can be earned by investing the proceeds of a short sale will vary with the circumstances of the short seller. If the short seller manages a long/short portfolio and is consistently short a substantial and varied portfolio, a significant fraction of the proceeds from these short sales can be invested in longer term instruments without concern over the need to sell the fixed income portfolio prematurely if a specific short is covered. Some portfolio short-sellers do receive short rebates based on term rates rather than an overnight rate.

In an effort to determine the effective cost of the stock loan process, we compared the Fed funds rate with the market rate for 90-day AA-rated commercial paper. The fed funds rate is an almost risk-free rate because the Fed, in effect, protects the lender from the credit risk of lending to the actual borrower of fed funds. Fluctuations in the fed funds rate largely reflect changes in the demand for reserve deposits within the Federal Reserve System. While letting a broker invest the proceeds of a short sale is not a high risk transaction, it is not comparable to "lending" to the Fed.

Brokers use the fed funds rate as a benchmark for the short rebate because it is a low risk (and, on average, low return) overnight rate. A more appropriate benchmark rate for many short selling portfolios is the rate on 90-day AA-rated commercial paper. The AA rating is at the high end of credit quality for investment banks, the credit in a short selling operation. The 90-day term is also more appropriate than an overnight rate for a rolling portfolio of short positions. The spread between 90-day AA commercial paper and Fed funds varies considerably over time, but the AA commercial paper rate is typically higher than the Fed funds rate. (See Figure 2.)

Figure 2: Daily Spread — 90-Day AA-Rated Commercial Paper Minus Federal Funds 1993-1996

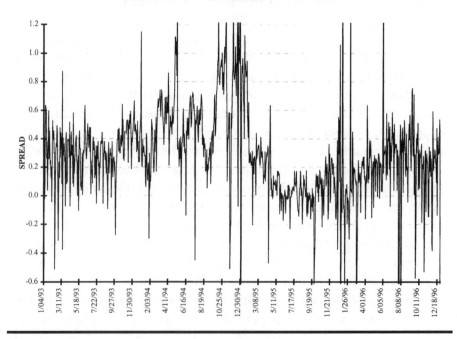

If we assume an average commercial paper rate premium of about 0.20% (20 basis points) over the Fed funds rate, the typical short rebate of fed funds less 25 basis points leaves the broker with 45 basis points (0.45%) to cover the costs of the stock loan process. The stock loan credit paid to the lender of a large capitalization stock may be 10 basis points or less — just enough to cover the stock lender's administrative costs plus a small profit. For simplicity, many brokers will pay short sellers a rebate of Fed funds less 25 basis points on all stocks, except for those that are the least liquid and, consequently, the hardest to borrow. Stocks which are very hard to borrow may carry no short rebate or, rarely, command a borrowing premium paid by the short seller.

OTHER ECONOMIC ISSUES

There are several other features of the synthetic short that affect its analysis by a would-be user of this alternative to the actual short sale. As with the synthetic long, the synthetic short has a nominal life which is fixed at the time the transaction is initiated. Typically, short sales are outstanding for a shorter time than long equity positions. Uncertainty about the length of time the investor will want to maintain a short position and uncertainty about a broker's ability to close the option position or to replace the synthetic short seller with another investor for the remaining life of the options, may lead to higher transaction costs for the synthetic short than for an actual short sale. Ordinarily these costs will be service charges rather than market impact costs, and they can be estimated in advance. We will return to this issue.

In contrast to a traditional short sale, the synthetic short seller does not face the risk of a buy in. This is particularly important in a hard-to-borrow stock. There is no stock lender in the immediate picture to demand return of the shares or force the synthetic short seller to cover. An Equity FLEX synthetic short position taken with European options provides automatic and complete buy in protection for the life of the options. If this buy in protection has any real value, it will be priced into the options that create the position. An interesting feature of synthetic shorts is that experienced short sellers may be among the creators of these positions. Seasoned short sellers may see an opportunity to extract a buy-in protection premium from less experienced short sellers who have an unjustified fear of buy-ins.

A relatively minor feature of Equity FLEX synthetic short positions is that they can be created without an uptick requirement.[6] This is unlikely to be a significant issue for several reasons. First, there are a variety of ways around the uptick requirement that are simpler than creating an Equity FLEX synthetic short position. For example, many dealers will sell in-the-money OTC puts for immediate or next day exercise to create an actual short position in a customer account. Exemption from the uptick rule is available to many dealers who have positions in the stock. This exemption will permit a dealer to sell a stock position from his inventory without an uptick as he creates the in-the-money puts. When the puts are exercised, the dealer's short put is replaced by the long stock position to replenish his inventory, and the account of the client who bought and exercised the put is short the stock. There are other option transactions using standardized or Equity FLEX options that can establish a short equivalent position more simply than creating a synthetic short if getting an uptick is the only issue.

TRANSACTION CHARGES AND THE COMPARATIVE ECONOMICS OF ACTUAL AND SYNTHETIC STOCK POSITIONS

Clearly, transaction charges affect the economics of synthetic stock. The principal competitive weakness of synthetic stock versus a transaction in the underlying shares is that the actual stock transaction takes place in a long established market where strongly competitive market forces have driven transaction costs to extraordinarily low levels. Because a synthetic stock position can be structured so that most of its transaction pricing is related to transaction pricing in the underlying stock, we can ignore market impact and trading spread differences. Spreads and market impact on multiple instruments will disappear because the synthetic will be priced off a transaction in the stock. On

---

[6] The "uptick rule" (17CFR240.10a) prohibits the short sale of a stock at a price that would create a downtick or be at the same price as the previous sale if the price on that sale was a downtick.

the other hand, brokerage charges and related fees for the synthetic will almost certainly be slightly higher than comparable fees for a stock trade, so the level of transaction charges and brokerage commissions becomes a critical issue in measuring the relative attractiveness of actual and synthetic positions. These charges will vary greatly from one account to another and any attempt to estimate or forecast costs for this specific application of Equity FLEX options is premature.

Our purpose, in any event, is to develop an analytical model, not to calculate costs on a specific trade. Consequently, we will simply assume for purposes of illustration that an account can take a synthetic long or short position for a transaction charge/brokerage commission of $0.03 per underlying share *more* than the net commission cost of buying or selling the actual shares. This $0.03 per share figure is arbitrary and the reader can substitute another cost figure if $0.03 proves to be too low or too high. The cost of closing out the synthetic position by exercise should be the same as the cost of closing out the stock position, but we assume that closing out the synthetic *early* will cost an additional $0.03 per underlying share. The higher cost of putting on and taking off a synthetic stock position relative to a traditional stock position gives a small, but clear transaction cost advantage to "real" stock.

The transaction cost advantage of actual stock can only be overcome by a carrying cost or return enhancement advantage for the synthetic. We can convert the hypothesized $0.03 per underlying share commission or fee difference to a basis point rate by assuming an average share price of $40. This brings the transaction charge difference to 7.5 basis points one way and 15 basis points round trip with an early closeout. These figures and estimates for gains from specific synthetic applications are illustrated in Table 1.

As the calculations in Table 1 suggest, different types of return enhancement pay off over different time periods and any advantage on the carry cost/return side of the equation must last long enough to overcome the transaction cost disadvantage of the synthetic. The maximum life of an Equity FLEX-based synthetic under current Exchange rules is five years; but many applications, especially on the short side, are relatively short term positions. An investor using synthetics must be sensitive to the probable holding period.

Table 1: The Comparative Economics of Actual and Synthetic Stock

	Hold for Term of Options		Close out Early	
	Value In Basis Points	Breakeven In Years	Value In Basis Points	Breakeven In Years
Transaction Fee Differential	7.5	—	15	—
Savings on Withholding Tax, 2% yield, 15% tax rate, (Long)	30	0.25	30	0.50
Enhanced Cash Investment Return (Long)	50	0.15	50	0.30
Avoid Stock Lending Costs (Short)	45	0.17	45	0.33

The potential withholding tax saving for foreign investors is relatively non-controversial and represents savings on a typical stock held by an investor resident in a treaty country. The stock loan cost savings on the short side may be available only if a trade can be crossed between a short seller and a long, or if the stock loan process can be avoided in some other way. The pricing of the synthetic by a dealer may offer less than 45 basis points to the synthetic short seller — part of the value of the cash enhancement opportunity may go to the dealer. Adding the possibilities, return enhancement opportunities should exceed 1% per year before transaction charges and dealer participation. Anything approaching this level of return enhancement should be large enough to stimulate interest in synthetics based on Equity FLEX options.

Several features of these trades are difficult to quantify in traditional ways. Investors who are interested in both avoiding the risk of buy-in on a short sale and receiving greater leverage with a long or short synthetic than might be available with actual stock may see additional advantages in the synthetic. The value of buy-in protection is highly subjective and should be evaluated on a case by case basis. While most large investors can obtain equivalent leverage with real stock or synthetics, investors with intermediate-sized portfolios — somewhere between a million dollar portfolio on the low side, and a very small hedge fund on the high side — might find the higher leverage financing available via synthetics to be particularly attractive. On the other hand, Equity FLEX option transaction charges are probably more sensitive than listed stock transactions to order size. Small and intermediate sized option orders bear higher costs and these orders may not be large enough for an initial opening Equity FLEX transaction (250 contracts/25,000 underlying shares or $1,000,000 worth of a $40 stock).[7] This large a position is probably beyond the interest of an investor who would find synthetic stock positions attractive for their leverage potential.

CONCLUSION

This analysis of the economics of actual versus synthetic stock is meant to be illustrative rather than definitive. While some users may find the synthetic position attractive on the economics alone, a far larger number will find the analysis useful in highlighting the source of costs and profit opportunities in pricing and implementing a trade. If the economics are competitive a trader can proceed on the basis of the principal tactical reason for using options — their asymmetric payout pattern. For most option users, the synthetic stock analyses will be simply an extension of traditional option evaluation, providing comfort that a position is in the fair value zone.

---

[7] If there is open interest in a specific Equity FLEX series, the minimum additional opening trades is 100 contracts. As few as 25 contracts may be traded in a closing transaction.

Chapter 6

Equity FLEX Procedures

This chapter provides a detailed description of the mechanics of Equity FLEX transactions. The institutional investor who wants to use Equity FLEX options in the management of a portfolio will contact a broker or dealer — much as he would initiate an OTC option trade. From the client's perspective, the interaction with the broker or dealer is similar to an OTC option trade, but the process is very different from the dealer's perspective. In the next section of this chapter we provide a brief description of the price discovery and trading process. This overview will help illustrate the advantage of the Equity FLEX process to the cost conscious investor. We provide more information or amplification on specific points and Equity FLEX procedures in the balance of this chapter.

INTRODUCTION TO EQUITY FLEX PROCEDURES

Once the client, alone or working with the broker or dealer, has developed an idea for an Equity FLEX transaction, the customer's broker telephones the order to the floor of the AMEX. The floor broker managing the order completes a request for quote (RFQ) form, describing the terms of the contracts for which bids and/or offers are being solicited. The broker representing the client is called the submitting member. If the submitting member is a dealer, the submitting firm may be prepared to cross a trade on the Exchange if its facilitating bid or offer is the best available.

The RFQ goes to the specialist responsible for options in the designated underlying stock and the specialist reviews it for completeness and accuracy. The Equity FLEX request must be for a minimum size of 250 contracts or the number of contracts overlying a $1 million position if the series is not currently open, or 100 contracts in an opening transaction if this series has already been traded and continues to be outstanding. Trades as small as 25 contracts (or any lesser number still outstanding) may take place to close out a position. Consulting the submitting member, the specialist fixes a request response time that can range from 2 to 20 minutes for responsive quotes to be reported to the post. A unique alphanumeric identifier is assigned to the request and the information on the proposed trade is disseminated over the Options Price Reporting Authority (OPRA) tape. This information will be displayed on special pages created for this purpose by leading quote vendors. At present this information is available from Bloomberg, ILX, Reuters, and Track Data. Potential Equity FLEX participants will see the RFQ announcement on the trading floor or from one of the data vendors which publish information on Equity FLEX RFQs. If they elect to do so, off floor dealers or their customers may prepare responsive bids or offers and send them to their brokers for representation to the specialist, who is responsible for maintaining the bids and offers on this proposed trade, consistent with the price and time priority rules of the Exchange.

Any participating member may modify his or her customer's responsive quote at any time during or at the end of the request response time. The submitting member also may enter a responsive bid or offer to facilitate the customer's trade. The submitting member's bid or offer ranks with any other bid or offer according to the price and time priority rules. If the submitting member indicates a desire to cross a trade, he is guaranteed the right to at least 25% of the non-customer side of the trade at the trade price. At the end of the response time, the best bid and offer (BBO) with size are disseminated over OPRA. The submitting member then must either accept or reject the BBO within a reasonable time period. The submitting member may accept all or part of the BBO subject to minimum requirements, reject the entire BBO, or attempt to negotiate a better price during a BBO improvement interval. Messages on revised BBOs will be disseminated as they change.

At the end of any BBO improvement interval, the submitting member must promptly accept or reject the BBO. If the entire BBO is not accepted, other participating members may accept any part of the unfilled balance, subject to minimum requirements. Trading may continue as long as there is interest on the floor. When the specialist determines that there is no further current interest in the specific

RFQ, he announces that the market is closed for that particular RFQ, and an administrative message to that effect is sent over OPRA. If a customer subsequently wishes to trade in this series, an entirely new RFQ must be submitted and the process repeated.

In some Equity FLEX trades, option terms such as premium, strike price and size will not be expressed as dollar amounts or number of contracts, but can be converted into these forms at the completion of the Equity FLEX trade. For example, the strike may be set at 10% over the last sale at time of trade or the premium may be reflected as a percentage of the underlying stock price. These terms are converted into dollar prices by the parties to the trade and disseminated over OPRA. If the terms cannot be specified in dollar amount and number of contracts immediately (for example, 10% out of the money puts on a $10 million notional amount based on the closing stock price), dissemination is made in notional and percentage terms agreed upon at the time of the trade. Once all contingent prices are determined, contract specifications are determined to the nearest eighth on strikes and on premiums above $3.00 and in sixteenths for premiums under $3.00. The midpoint of a price range is rounded up.

Any member of the Exchange can participate in Equity FLEX transactions. The specialist in the option is required to provide a bid, an offer or both (depending on the terms of the RFQ), but other participating members in the Equity FLEX process are not required to respond to a given RFQ. Members who do respond are required to respond for at least 100 contracts (25 contracts for a closing transaction). To avoid contributing to the crush of OPRA tape traffic at the 9:30 opening of option trading, Equity FLEX trading hours are 10:00 a.m. to 4:00 p.m., New York time.

This brief summary of the trading process will be adequate for most customers and some brokers. The rest of this chapter offers a more comprehensive discussion of each step and clearly labeled sections with answers to frequently asked questions.

AN EQUITY FLEX OPERATIONS GUIDE

This section provides a step-by-step explanation of the trading procedures for Equity FLEX options on the American Stock Exchange and user-friendly summaries of key rule provisions. Other exchanges which trade Equity FLEX options operate under similar rules, although their procedures may vary slightly. Several exhibits and examples are offered to help the reader understand how Equity FLEX options trade.

Stocks and Index Shares Eligible for Equity FLEX Trading

Any stock or Index Share eligible for standardized options trading can become eligible for Equity FLEX Options trading.[1] Currently, AMEX only trades Equity FLEX options on stocks and Index Shares listed for standardized options trading on the AMEX. If you are not sure that an underlying stock is on the OCC's Equity FLEX list, contacting the service desk with your indication of possible interest well before 1:00 p.m. will assure you of the opportunity to trade later in the day. If the OCC does not receive an indication of interest in trading an Equity FLEX option on a stock that has not yet been listed for Equity FLEX trading prior to 1:00 p.m. New York time, there may be a one-day processing delay at the OCC to add the stock or Index Share. If a multiply-listed option stock has been qualified with the OCC by any exchange, it is eligible for Equity FLEX trading on all participating options exchanges.

Flexible Terms

Expiration Date

An expiration date can be any business day three years or less from the trade date which does not fall within two business days of a third-Friday expiration (i.e., Wednesday, Thursday, expiration Friday, Monday, Tuesday). If an Exchange official determines that there is sufficient liquidity in longer options on the stock, the life of an Equity FLEX option may be as long as 5 years. Trade day expiration for a *newly created series* is not allowed; but expiration day trades, both opening and closing, are possible in a previously traded series with a remaining open interest. Invalid expiration dates through 2003 are listed in Table 1. You can trade an Equity FLEX option *expiring on any date not on this list*.

---

[1] Approximately 2,500 stocks traded on the AMEX, the NYSE or through Nasdaq currently are the subject of standardized options trading with approximately 800 new option stocks added in each of 1996 and 1997.

Table 1: Invalid Equity FLEX Expiration Dates

1998

January		May		September	
1,3,4		2,3		5,6	
10,11		9,10		7,12,13	
14,15,16,17,18		13,14,15,16,17		16,17,18,19,20	
19,20, 21, 24,25		18,19,23,24		21,22,26,27	
31		25,30,31			
February		**June**		**October**	
1		6,7		3,4	
7,8		13,14		10,11	
14,15		17,18,19,20,21		14,15,16,17,18	
16,18,19,20,21,22		22,23,27,28		19,20,24,25	
23,24,28				31	
March		**July**		**November**	
1		3,4,5		1	
7,8		11,12		7,8	
14,15		15,16,17,18,19		14,15	
18,19,20,21,22		20,21,25,26		18,19,20,21,22	
23,24,28,29				23,24,26,28,29	
April		**August**		**December**	
4,5		1,2		5,6	
10,11,12		8,9		12,13	
15,16,17,18,19		15,16		16,17,18,19,20	
20,21,25,26		19,20,21,22,23		21,22,25,26,27	
		24,25,29,30			

1999

January		May		September	
1,2		1		4	
3,9		2,8		5,6,11	
10,13,14,15,16		9,15		12,15,16,17,18	
17,18,19, 20, 23		16,19,20,21,22		19,20,21,25	
24,30		23,24,25,29		26	
31		30,31			
February		**June**		**October**	
6		5		2	
7,13		6,12		3,9	
14,15,17,18,19,20		13,16,17,18,19		10,13,14,15,16	
21,22,23,27		20,21,22,26		17,18,19,23	
28		27		24,30	
				31	
March		**July**		**November**	
6		3		6	
7,13		4,5,10		7,13	
14,17,18,19,20		11,14,15,16,17		14,17,18,19,20	
21,22,23,27		18,19,20,24		21,22,23,25,27	
28		25,31		28	
April		**August**		**December**	
2,3		1,7		4	
4,10		8,14		5,11	
11,14,15,16,17		15,18,19,20,21		12,15,16,17,18	
18,19,20,24		22,23,24,28		19,20,21,24,25	
25		29		26	

Table 1 (Continued)

2000

Month	Dates	Month	Dates	Month	Dates
January	1,2 8,9,15 16,17,19,20,21,22 23,24,25,29,30	May	6 7,13 14,17 18,19,20,21,22 23,27,28,29	September	2 3,4,9 10,13,14,15,16 17,18,19,23 24,30
February	5 6,12 13,16,17,18,19,20 21,22,23,26 27	June	3 4,10 11,14,15,16,17 18,19,20,24 25	October	1 7,8 14,15,18,19,20 21,22,23,24,28 29
March	4 5,11 12,15,16,17,18 19,20,21,25 26	July	1,2 4,8,9 15,16,19,20,21 22,23,24,25 29,30	November	4 5,11 12,15,16,17,18 19,20,21,23,25 26
April	1,2 8,9 15,16,18,19,20 21,22,23,24,25 29,30	August	5,6 12,13 16,17,18,19,20 21,22,26,27	December	2 3,9 10,13,14,15,16 17,18,19,23,24,25 30,31

2001

Month	Dates	Month	Dates	Month	Dates
January	1,6 7,13 14,15,17,18,19,20 21,22,23,27 28	May	5 6,12 13,16,17,18,19 20,21,22,26 27,28	September	1 2,3,8 9,15 16,19,20,21,22 23,24,25,29 30
February	3 4,10 11,14,15,16,17 18,19,20,21,24 25	June	2 3,9 10,13,14,15,16 17,18,19,23 24,30	October	6, 7,13 14,17,18,19,20 21,22,23,27 28
March	3 4,10 11,14,15,16,17 18,19,20,24 25,31	July	1,4,7 8,14 15,18,19,20,21 22,23,24,28 29	November	3 4,10 11,14,15,16,17 18,19,20,22,24 25
April	1,7 8,13,14 15,18,19,20,21 22,23,24,28 29	August	4 5,11 12,15,16,17,18 19,20,21,25 26	December	1 2,8 9,15 16,19,20,21,22 23,24,25,26,29,30

Table 1 (Continued)

2002

Month	Days
January	1,5 / 6,12 / 13,16,17,18,19 / 20,21,22,23,26 / 27
February	2 / 3,9 / 10,13,14,15,16 / 17,18,19,20,23 / 24
March	2 / 3,9 / 10,13,14,15,16 / 17,18,19,23 / 24,29,30 / 31
April	6 / 7,13 / 14,17,18,19,20 / 21,22,23,27 / 28
May	4 / 5,11 / 12,15,16,17,18 / 19,20,21,25 / 26,27
June	1 / 2,8 / 9,15 / 16,19,20,21,22 / 23,24,25,29,30
July	4,6 / 7,13 / 14,17,18,19,20 / 21,22,23,27 / 28
August	3 / 4,10 / 11,14,15,16,17 / 18,19,20,24 / 25,31
September	1,2,7 / 8,14 / 15,18,19,20,21 / 22,23,24,28 / 29
October	5 / 6,12 / 13,16,17,18,19 / 20,21,22,26 / 27
November	2 / 3,9 / 10,13,14,15,16 / 17,18,19,23 / 24,28,30
December	1,7 / 8,14 / 15,18,19,20,21 / 22,23,24,25,28 / 29

2003

Month	Days
January	1,4 / 5,11 / 12,15,16,17,18 / 19,20,21,22,25 / 26
February	1 / 2,8 / 9,15 / 16,17,19,20,21,22 / 23,24,25
March	1 / 2,8 / 9,15 / 16,19,20,21,22 / 23,24,25,29 / 30
April	5 / 6,12 / 13,15,16,17,18,19 / 20,21,22,26 / 27
May	3 / 4,10 / 11,14,15,16,17 / 18,19,20,24 / 25,26,31
June	1,7 / 8,14 / 15,18,19,20,21 / 22,23,24,28 / 29
July	4,5 / 6,12 / 13,16,17,18,19 / 20,21,22,26 / 27
August	2 / 3,9 / 10,13,14,15,16 / 17,18,19,23 / 24,30,31
September	1,6 / 7,13 / 14,17,18,19,20 / 21,22,23,27 / 28
October	4 / 5,11 / 12,15,16,17,18 / 19,20,21,25 / 26
November	1 / 2,8 / 9,15 / 16,19,20,21,22 / 23,24,25,27,29 / 30
December	6 / 7,13 / 14,17,18,19,20 / 21,22,23,25,27 / 28

Exercise Style

The exercise style can be American (any business day up to and including expiration day) or European (expiration day only). All Equity FLEX options positions that remain open at expiration are physically settled at the close on the expiration day, which is also the last trading day for the option.

Exercise Price

For *calls* the strike prices may be set *only* at standard intervals[2] — generally 2½ points for strike prices of $25 or less; 5 points for strike prices over $25 through $200; and 10 points for strike prices over $200. Option classes which are part of a 2½ strike price pilot program may also have Equity FLEX strike prices at 2½-point intervals for strike prices in the range of $25 to $50. (See Table 2 for a current list of these classes. The 2½-point strike program is being expanded so this list will grow.) *Call strikes on Equity FLEX options on Index Shares can be at any eighth point interval because options on Index Shares are not deemed eligible for qualified covered call treatment.*

For *puts* strike prices are limited only by the requirement that a calculated strike price be rounded to the nearest eighth. Strike prices can be based on a numerical relationship or a percentage value of the underlying stock.

Quotation and Trading Procedures

Because of its unique nature, the Equity FLEX program operates under a modified version of the AMEX specialist system. Every effort has been made to keep the operation as consistent with current practice on standardized equity options as possible. Selected AMEX staff have been trained to assist market participants in trading Equity FLEX options, to ensure that information is disseminated properly, and to ensure that the entire process runs smoothly.

Initiating the Bid/Offer Process

Although the steps in effecting an Equity FLEX transaction are listed in roughly sequential order, several steps may occur at the same

---

[2] In June 1998, the IRS proposed a new regulation for qualified covered calls which, if implemented, will clear the way for full flexibility in setting call strike prices for Equity FLEX options at one-eighth point intervals. See the discussion of this problem in Appendix B.

time. Several examples of actual Equity FLEX messages provided in Table 5 may help the reader understand some of the timing issues and procedures in Equity FLEX.

Table 2: Two and One-Half Point Strike Price Pilot Program (as of 8/6/98)

Selected Option Issues	Exchanges Where Listed
3COM Corporation	P
AccuStaff Inc.	C
Adaptec, Inc.	A
Advanced Micro Devices	P
Ahmanson (H.F.) & Company	A
ALZA Corporation	P
Anheuser Busch Companies Inc.	X
Apple Computer	A
Applied Materials, Inc.	P
ASA Limited	A
Atmel Corp.	A,C
Baker Hughes, Inc.	P
Banc One Corp.	P
Bay Networks, Inc.	C
Bed, Bath & Beyond, Inc.	C
Biochem Pharma, Inc.	C,P
Boeing Co.	C
Burlington Resources Co.	X
CBS Corporation	A
Charles Schwab Corporation	C
Chrysler Corporation	C
Circus Enterprises, Inc.	A
CNF Transportation, Inc.	C
Coca-Cola Enterprises, Inc.	C
Columbia/HCA Healthcare Corporation	A,C
Comair Holdings, Inc.	C
Comcast Corp. Special Class A	X
Compaq Computer Corp.	P
Corning Inc.	C
CUC International Inc.	X
Cummins Engine Company, Inc.	C
Data General Corporation	P
Digital Equipment Corporation	A
Disney (Walt) Company	A,C
DSC Communications Corporation	A
Electronic Data Systems Corp.	X
EMC Corp.	C

Table 2 (Continued)

Selected Option Issues	Exchanges Where Listed
Federal Home Loan Mortgage Corporation	A
Federated Department Stores, Inc.	C
Ford Motor Corporation	C
Glaxo Wellcome P.L.C.	A
Global Marine, Inc.	A,C,P
GPU, Inc.	C
Grupo Televisa, S.A. de C.V.	A,C
GTE Corporation	A
Hilton Hotels Corporation	P
Humana, Inc.	C
Ingersoll-Rand Company	C
Jones Medical Industries	C
KCS Energy, Inc.	P
Key Energy Group, Inc.	P,X
Loral Space & Communications, Ltd.	C
Lowe's Companies Inc.	X
Mattel, Inc.	A
McDonalds Corp	C
MCI Communications	C
Micron Technology Inc.	C,P
National Semiconductor Corp.	C
Newmont Mining Corp.	X
Nynex Corp.	C
Octel Communications Corporation	P
Oracle Corporation	C
Oryx Energy	A,C,X
Parametric Technology	X
Patriot American Hospitality, Inc.	X
Paychex, Inc.	X
Pep Boys Manny Moe & Jack	C
PepsiCo. Inc.	C
Philip Morris Companies, Inc.	A
Phillips Petroleum Company	A
PNC Bank Corp.	X
Quaker Oats company	X
Quantum Corp.	C
QWEST Communications International	A,C,X
Republic Industries, Inc.	A,C
RJR Nabisco Holdings Corp.	A,C,X
Rubbermaid Inc.	P
Seagate Technology Inc.	A
Seagram Ltd.	P

Table 2 (Continued)

Selected Option Issues	Exchanges Where Listed
Solectron Corporation	C
Staples, Inc.	X
Starbucks Corp.	C
Summit Bancorp	C
Sun Microsystems, Inc.	P
Sysco Corporation	C
Telefonica De Argentina S.A.	A,C,P
Teredyne, Inc.	P
Union Carbide Corporation	A
United States Surgical Corporation	A
Unocal Corp.	P
US West Inc.	A
USG Corp.	C
USX-U.S. Steel Group	A
USX Marathon Group (MRO)	A
VLSI Technology, Inc.	A,C
Wal-Mart Stores Inc.	C
Witco Corporation	C
WMX Technologies Inc.	X
World Com, Inc.	P
Xylan Corporation	A,C,P

Step 1. To initiate the FLEX bid and offer process, an Exchange member must submit a "Request For Quote" (RFQ) in proper form to the appropriate AMEX option specialist. The specialist for Equity FLEX options on a given security is the specialist in standard options on the security. A copy of a blank RFQ form appears as Figure 1. The member who brings the RFQ to the floor — referred to as the "Submitting Member" for this transaction — completes the top portion of the RFQ which describes the terms of the contract for which bids and/or offers are being solicited. The RFQ includes:

> *Option symbol*: Must be an option on a stock or an Index Share on which AMEX currently trades standardized equity options. If the OCC has not been notified previously to be prepared to clear Equity FLEX trades on this underlying stock, OCC must be notified by 1:00 p.m. on the day of the proposed trade.

Figure 1: RFQ Form

American
Stock Exchange

86 Trinity Place
New York, New York 10006-1881

Equity FLEX
RFQ/Trade Ticket

RFQ#	Response Time:

Request For Quote:

Member's Name_____

Badge # _____ Date _____ Time ____

Option Symbol _____ Buy/Sell   Call/Put

Expiration Date _____   Amer/Euro

Strike Price: Price/Percent _____

Req Size: Contracts/$Amt _____ Spread/Cross

Comments:

Trade Information: Size: Contracts/$Amt _____

Premium: Price/Percent _____ Time _____

Exec CM _____ Contra CM _____ Contra Badge _____

O/C   Acct Type: C/F/M   MMID _____ CMTA _____

Optional Data:

The AMEX will convert, as necessary, percentages and notional values into dollar amounts and
number of contracts based on the best available information at the specified time, but does not
guarantee the accuracy of such information. The parities are responsible for verifying these
conversions either after the close of trading that day or from OCC reports the following day. Any
corrections must be brought to the attention of the AMEX immediately.

AMEX

Expiration date: Maximum contract term of three years (five years with the approval of an Exchange official); minimum of one day if a newly created series. Trade day expiration is permitted in previously traded and still open series only. Expiration date cannot be a weekend or a holiday, and it cannot be within two business days of a standard options expiration date (typically the third Friday of the month). A 5-year calendar of invalid dates appears as Table 1.[3]

---

[3] Updates may be obtained by calling 1-800-THE-AMEX.

Requested Size: Minimum size requirement of
- 250 contracts or, if less, the number of contracts overlying a $1 million position if the series currently is not open.
- 100 contracts (or remaining open interest on a closing transaction) if the series currently is open; except that a trade may occur for as few as 25 contracts as long as one side of the trade is closing out part of an existing position, or less than 25 contracts as long as one side of the trade is closing out an entire existing position.[4]

Contract type:
- Option type indicated as call or put.
- "Spread" indication marked if part of combination trade.[5]
- "Cross" indication marked if submitting member intends to cross trade and wishes to be guaranteed at least 25% of trade.[6]

Exercise type: Option style is American or European.

Strike price: Appropriate exercise price is specified (as dollar price or percentage of underlying stock price). Note the limitation on eligible call strikes to standard strikes as described above.

Type of Quote Requested:
- Quote type requested (buy, sell, or both).
- Quote form that is acceptable and understandable (dollar amount, percentage of underlying price, other).

Comments: Any additional information pertaining to the terms of the RFQ — may be a clarification or restatement of terms

---

[4] Current Open Series information is available every business day from 1-800-THE-AMEX.

[5] Spread trades and other combination trades require separate RFQs for each leg and require that the "spread indication" be circled on all related RFQs. Thus, the RFQs are linked in an "all or nothing" manner and are assigned the same RFQ identifier. A single RFQ message will go out to vendors over the Options Price Reporting Authority (OPRA) wire indicating the terms of the desired spread/combination as a single trade. Similarly, the responsive quotes will be on a net basis, as will the trade price. The terms of the individual legs of the RFQ will be "backed out" by the specialist and counterparties when the trade is done.

[6] Sharing/crossing of trades among FLEX participants will be handled by the same rules currently in place for standard options — except that the Submitting Member who indicates an intention to cross at the time of the RFQ is entitled to at least 25% of the trade.

already indicated on the form, such as a description of a spread transaction; or it may be additional terms not already indicated elsewhere on the RFQ, such as a delta neutral trade with stock, a stock price limit on a covered call write, etc.

Step 2. When he receives the RFQ, the specialist sets the Request Response Time — the time by which responsive quotes from market makers and brokers must be given to the specialist (currently this can be between 2 and 20 minutes) — and alerts the AMEX FLEX staff to the request.

Step 3. AMEX FLEX staff validates the RFQ terms and assigns a unique alphanumeric identifier to the RFQ. RFQ identifiers are assigned sequentially to all RFQs of the same class, beginning each day with, for example, AAQ1 for the first Apple request of the day, MO1 for the first Philip Morris request, etc. Subsequent messages regarding quotes and trades for this request carry this identifier.

Step 4. AMEX FLEX staff disseminates the RFQ information over OPRA to data vendors (see "OPRA Dissemination").

Step 5. The specialist announces the RFQ terms to the trading crowd.

Step 6. Potential Equity FLEX participants who are in the trading crowd, who see the RFQ announcement on a quote vendor's screen, or upstairs traders and investors who learn about the RFQ from a representative on the floor or a market data vendor's screen may prepare responsive bids and offers.

Step 7. Bids and offers (with size) are given to the specialist, who is responsible for maintaining the inside market (BBO) with size in accordance with the time and price priority rules of the Exchange. Any member may modify his responsive quote (bid, offer, and/or size) at any point during or at the end of the Request Response Time.

Step 8. At the end of the Request Response Time, the specialist gives the AMEX FLEX staff the BBO with size for dissemination over OPRA. The submitting member must accept or reject the BBO within a "reasonable" time period.

Step 9. At the end of the Request Response Time, the submitting member may accept all or part of the BBO (subject to minimum trade size requirements), may reject the entire BBO, or may attempt to negotiate a better price during a "BBO Improvement Interval." The BBO Improvement Interval is a period during which Equity FLEX participants may modify their responsive quotes to better an existing market established during an initial Request Response Time. Any BBO Improvement Interval is determined by the specialist and may be kept open until there is no further interest in the requested market. The specialist may alert the AMEX FLEX staff to disseminate OPRA messages for the revised BBO as it changes.

Step 10. At the end of any BBO Improvement Interval, the submitting member must promptly accept or reject the BBO.

Step 11. Whenever the submitting member does not accept the entire BBO, participating members may accept any part of the unfilled balance in accordance with AMEX rules and procedures.

Step 12. When the specialist determines that there is no further interest in the RFQ, he announces to the crowd that the market is "closed" for that particular RFQ and alerts the AMEX FLEX staff, which sends an administrative message to that effect over OPRA. If a member wants to reopen the market for that Equity FLEX contract, he must submit a new RFQ.

Step 13. In the event of a trade, terms are recorded by each party on the bottom portion of the RFQ. Parameters such as premium, strike price, and size which are not expressed as dollar amounts or number of contracts but which can be converted into these forms at this time are converted by the parties to the trade. AMEX FLEX staff disseminates information on the trade over OPRA. If the trade parameters cannot be converted to dollars until after the market close, the conversion is part of post-trade processing.

Post-Trade Processing

As with standard equity options, Equity FLEX trades are compared via AMEX's IDC (Intraday Comparison) facility. Buyers and sellers enter trade information into IDC for comparison through a special Equity FLEX function. *Information must be entered and compared prior to 4:30 p.m. for Equity FLEX transactions.* After 4:30, participants will be able to view the details of their Equity FLEX activity for the day, but will not be able to modify or correct any of the information. Uncompared trades will generate notices the next morning which must be resolved by the members. Uncompared trades which expire the same day, *cannot be resolved the following morning*; therefore, it is important that the trade parties ensure that such a trade is compared that day.

Where terms of a trade cannot be specified in dollar amount and number of contracts immediately after execution (e.g., 250 10% out-of-the-money calls based on the closing stock price for the day), comparison information is entered into IDC using percentage terms agreed upon at the time of trade. The AMEX will convert percentages and notional values into dollar amounts (for calls, to nearest strike price corresponding to a standardized listed call option on the underlying security and for puts, to the nearest eighth for strike price and premium above $3, $\frac{1}{16}$ rounds up; to nearest sixteenth of premium under $3, $\frac{1}{32}$ rounds up) and number of contracts (0.5 rounds up) at the end of the day, based on best available information. *The trade parties are responsible for verifying these conversions either after the close of trading that day or from OCC reports the following morning.* Any corrections must be brought to the attention of the AMEX staff immediately.

Like standard options, Equity FLEX trades will appear in a firm's contract sheets from the OCC the next day.

OPRA Dissemination

Equity FLEX quote and sale information is disseminated via administrative text messages directly over OPRA in conventional format. These messages will be picked up by market data vendors for their Equity FLEX Option displays. Bloomberg, ILX, Reuters and Track Data presently carry Equity FLEX information. The specific key strokes used to view Equity FLEX information on each of the different vendors are detailed in Table 3.

Table 3: Equity FLEX Option Vendor Keystrokes

Bloomberg:
  FLEX [Go]
       Page display of all FLEX messages (Equity and Index) for all exchanges.
  FLXD [Go]
       Allows user to filter out messages to be displayed by FLEX [Go] function. User may select by
       type (Index vs. Equity) and/or exchange.

ILX:
       Available through Market Pulse/Business Pulse display.
       [F12] pulls up Market Pulse page.
       Enter **FLEX** on command line to all FLEX messages (Equity and Index) for all exchanges. Must hit
       [Enter] to update information once page has been accessed.

Track Data:
  .FLEX [News Recall]
       Page display of all FLEX messages (Equity and Index) for all exchanges.
       To view full text of E-FLEX message which has been truncated, highlight desired message
       using down arrow key and press **[Insert]** key.

Reuters America, Inc.:
  TST/FLXA[Enter]
       Scrolling list of most recent Equity FLEX Options activity for all exchanges.
  TST/FLXB - Z[Enter]
       Today's history of Equity FLEX Options activity for all exchanges.

There are five different basic types of Equity FLEX options messages, each of which is discussed in greater detail below. In all cases, the message adheres to the format in Table 4.

RFQ (Request for Quote) Message The RFQ message announces the terms of a specific quote request and indicates the "RFQ Identifier" associated with that request. Following is an example:

Product Type	4	FLEX
Filler	1	(SPACE)
FLEX Type	1	E
Filler	1	(SPACE)
Security Symbol	3	TBR
Filler	1	(SPACE)
Message type	3	RFQ
Filler	1	(SPACE)
Request Identifier	5	TBR1(SPACE)
Filler	1	(SPACE)
Variable Message Text	53	CALL 12/31/98 105% EUR $500 QUOTE IN % BY 1030 EST

Table 4: Types of Equity FLEX Option Messages

Description	Length	Type	Details
Product Type	4	Alpha Characters	FLEX
Filler	1	SPACE	
FLEX Type	1	Alpha Character	I for Index, E for Equity
Filler	1	SPACE	
Security Symbol	3	Alpha Characters	1-3 characters, left justified, space filled
Filler	1	SPACE	
Message Type	3	Alpha Characters	RFQ – Request for Quote QTE – Quote LST – Last Sale IND – Indicative Quote ADM – Administrative Text Message
Filler	1	SPACE	
Request Identifier	5	Alphanumeric Characters	2-5 characters space filled, left justified. (Not present in IND messages; may not be present in ADM messages)
Filler	1	SPACE	
Variable Message Text	variable	Alphanumeric Characters	FLEX "E" LST message has additional structure defined below

This message is an Equity FLEX Request for Quote on a Telebras (TBR) call, expiration date 12/31/98, strike price 5% out-of-the-money, European expiration, 500 contracts. Quotes must be made as a percentage of the stock price and must be in by 10:30 Eastern Standard Time.

QTE (Quote) Message The QTE message displays the quoted best bid and offer market, with size, for the specific RFQ, as indicated by RFQ identifier. An example of a QTE message follows:

Product Type	4	FLEX
Filler	1	(SPACE)
FLEX Type	1	E
Filler	1	(SPACE)
Security Symbol	3	INQ
Filler	1	(SPACE)
Message Type	3	QTE
Filler	1	(SPACE)
Request Identifier	5	INQ12
Filler	1	(SPACE)
Variable Message Text	42	4½%-5% 1000 × 1000

This message is an Equity FLEX Quote for Intel, according to the terms of the request assigned identifier INQ12. Bid 4½% of stock price – offer 5% of stock price, size 1,000 contracts to buy or sell. Note that QTE messages do not state whether the option is a put or call. That information is in the referenced RFQ.

LST (Last Sale/Trade) Message The LST message displays the price and size of an Equity FLEX transaction associated with a specific RFQ along with certain clearing information regarding the trade. Unlike the other message types, the LST message has a specific format. In the case of spread or combination trades, an administrative message with the net price of the trade is first disseminated as an ADM message. Then the terms of the separate legs are disseminated via LST messages. Following is an example of an LST message:

Product Type	4	FLEX
Filler	1	(SPACE)
FLEX Type	1	E
Filler	1	(SPACE)
Security Symbol	3	AAQ
Filler	1	(SPACE)
Message Type	3	LST
Filler	1	(SPACE)
Request Identifier	5	AAQ5(SPACE)
Filler	1	(SPACE)
Strike Price	1-9	25
Filler	1	(SPACE)
Type (call or put)	1	C
Filler	1	(SPACE)
Exercise Style (Amer, Eur)	3-4	AMER
Filler	1	(SPACE)
Expiration Date	10	02.02.1999
Filler	1	(SPACE)
Volume	5	500
Filler	3	(SPACE)@(SPACE)
Premium	1-9	3⅝
Filler	1	(SPACE)
Clearing Symbol	6	1AAQ02

This message is an Equity FLEX Last Sale for Apple Computer, 25 strike calls, American exercise, expiring on 2/2/99. 500 calls traded at 3⅝.

IND (Indicative Quote) Message The IND message may be used to display an indicative quote for an Equity FLEX Option series — to ascertain potential market pricing and generate interest in an anticipated new series — when an RFQ has not been requested for that series. An indicative quote is not firm— a trade can only occur in response to an RFQ. An example of an IND message follows:

Product Type	4	FLEX
Filler	1	(SPACE)
FLEX Type	1	E
Filler	1	(SPACE)
Security Symbol	3	MO(SPACE)
Filler	1	(SPACE)
Message type	3	IND
Filler	1	(SPACE)
Variable Message Text	53	2YR ATMC 18.55%-18.63%

This message is an Equity FLEX Indicative Quote for a Phillip Morris 2-year at-the-money call. Indicated at 18.55% bid, 18.63% offered.

ADM (Administrative Text) Message The ADM message type is free format text to disseminate general administrative messages pertaining to Equity FLEX options, such as corrections or clarifications of previous messages, or indications of number of Equity FLEX trades on a given day and number of Equity FLEX contracts traded on a given day. This message also is used to announce the close of an RFQ once the specialist has determined that there is no further interest. Following is an example of an ADM message:

Product Type	4	FLEX
Filler	1	(SPACE)
FLEX Type	1	E
Filler	1	(SPACE)
Security Symbol	3	MO(SPACE)
Filler	1	(SPACE)
Message type	3	ADM
Filler	1	(SPACE)
Variable Message Text	53	RFQ MO1 Market Closed

This message is an Equity FLEX Administrative Message that RFQ MO1 has been closed.

Table 5 provides several examples of actual Equity FLEX messages. Although several Requests for Quotes may occur at the same time, with messages intertwined, we have separated each transaction here for purposes of clarity.

In the first example, a Request for Quote in Ingram Micro, Inc. (ticker symbol: IM) is disseminated at 12:18. This is the second RFQ in Ingram Micro, Inc. for the day, as represented by the identifier IM2. The request is for 1000 American-style calls at an exercise price of $65, with an expiration date of June 4, 2001. The requester would like a quote in dollars by 12:20, just two minutes later. At 12:20, the quote is disseminated — the bid price is $4⅞ and the offer price is $5⅛. Both the bid and offer prices are good for 1000 contracts. At 12:22, the tape reports that a trade in the option took place for 1000 contracts at a price of $5⅛. The clearing symbol for the option is 1IM04. Finally, at 12:23 the tape reports that the market is closed for this RFQ. If a customer wishes to do another trade in this option, he must submit a new RFQ, as in the second example.

At 1:00 p.m., another RFQ arrives for the same option, requesting quotes by 1:03. Rather than repeating all of the terms of the request, the new RFQ simply references the original terms using the message "SEE RFQ 2". The quote arrives at 1:03 and another trade occurs on the same terms as before.

In the third example, an RFQ arrives at 2:29 for 500 straddles (puts and calls together with the same exercise price of $110) on Telebras (ticker symbol: TBR) with American-style exercise by October 13, 1998. The responsive quote is requested by 2:31. At 2:31, the tape carries the best quote of $26½ bid and $28 offered, good to buy or sell 1000 contracts. Note that the quoted size is larger than requested in the RFQ. At 2:33, the administrative message announces a trade of 750 straddles at a combined price of $27. The two subsequent last sale (LST) messages contain the details of the call and put legs of the straddle. Note that there remains an additional 250 straddles that are bid and offered for after the transaction. At 2:37, the tape reports that an additional transaction for the remaining 250 straddles occurs at the same price. With no more interest left after the second trade, the market for this RFQ is closed.

Table 5: Equity Flex Options Sample Messages

Time	Exchange		Stock Symbol	Type of Message	RFQ Identifier	Message Text
12:18	AMEX	E	IM	RFQ	IM2	100 65 C AMER 06.04.01 IN $ BY 12:20
12:20	AMEX	E	IM	QTE	IM2	4 7/8 - 5 1/8 1000 x 1000
12:22	AMEX	E	IM	LST	IM2	65 C AMER 06.04.2001 1000 @ 5 1/8 1IM 04
12:23	AMEX	E	IM	ADM	IM2	MKT CLOSED
13:00	AMEX	E	IM	RFQ	IM3	SEE RFQ 2 IN $ BY 1:03
13:03	AMEX	E	IM	QTE	IM3	4 7/8 - 5 1/8 1000 x 1000
13:05	AMEX	E	IM	LST	IM3	65 C AMER 06.04.2001 1000 @ 5 1/8 1 IM 04
13:25	AMEX	E	IM	ADM	IM3	MKT CLOSED
14:29	AMEX	E	TBR	RFQ	TBR1	500 OCT 110 STRADDLE C/P AMER 10.13.98 IN $ BY 2:31
14:31	AMEX	E	TBR	QTE	TBR1	26 1/2 - 28 1000 x 1000
14:33	AMEX	E	TBR	ADM	TBR1	750 OCT 110 STRADDLE @ 27 LAST SALE
14:35	AMEX	E	TBR	LST	TBR1	110 C AMER 10.13.1998 750 @ 14 1TBR13
14:35	AMEX	E	TBR	LST	TBR1	110 P AMER 10.13.1998 750 @ 13 1TBR13
14:37	AMEX	E	TBR	ADM	TBR1	250 OCT 110 STRADDLE @ 27 LAST SALE
14:38	AMEX	E	TBR	LST	TBR1	110 P AMER 10.13.1998 250 @ 13 1TBR13
14:38	AMEX	E	TBR	LST	TBR1	110 C AMER 10.13.1998 250 @ 14 1TBR13
14:40	AMEX	E	TBR	ADM	TBR1	MKT CLOSED
11:28	AMEX	E	TBR	RFQ	TBR1	1500 115 C AMER 8.10.98 DELTA NEUT VS STK IN$BY 11:30
11:30	AMEX	E	TBR	QTE	TBR1	4 3/4 - 5 3/4 1500 x 1500
11:31	AMEX	E	TBR	ADM	TBR1	55,500 @104 3/8 STOCK
11:31	AMEX	E	TBR	LST	TBR1	115 C AMER 08.10.1998 945 @4 7/8 1TBR10
11:32	AMEX	E	TBR	LST	TBR1	115 C AMER 08.10.1998 555 @4 3/4 1TBR10
11:35	AMEX	E	TBR	ADM	TBR1	5600 @104 3/16 STOCK
11:35	AMEX	E	TBR	LST	TBR1	115 C AMER 08.10.1998 140 @4 3/4 1TBR10
11:35	AMEX	E	TBR	LST	TBR1	115 C AMER 08.10.1998 10 @4 7/8 1TBR10
11:45	AMEX	E	TBR	ADM	TBR1	MKT CLOSED

The final example contains an RFQ from the following day in Telebras. As the first RFQ for that day in TBR, the RFQ identifier associated with this transaction is TBR1, the same as in the previous example, which was the first TBR transaction on the previous day. In Equity FLEX options, RFQ identifiers begin at 1 each day. This request is for a quote on 1500 American-style call expiring on August 10, 1998 with an exercise price of $115. This trade is part of a "delta-neutral" strategy in which the investor trades the options and the underlying shares at the same time so that the investor's position is approximately unaffected by relatively small changes in the stock price. Note that the 1500 contracts traded are reported in two pieces at slightly different prices, to arrive at an overall transaction price more precise that the ⅛ minimum increments of Equity FLEX trades. An administrative text message also lists the number and price of TBR common shares that traded as part of this transaction. After this transaction is completed, there is sufficient additional interest to result in an additional 150 contracts trading. Afterwards, the market is reported closed for the RFQ.

FLEX Administration/Rules
Standard equity option rules apply, except for the following:

Trading hours: 10:00 a.m. through 4:00 p.m. New York time.

Position limits: None.

Reporting requirements: Each AMEX member must file a report (Figure 2) with the Exchange when an account is carrying an Equity FLEX option position in excess of three times the position limit for standardized options on that stock. Based on this report, the OCC will perform a risk evaluation of the account and its position, and may impose additional margin.

Expiration processing: As with standardized equity options, standard "exercise by exception" processing applies, but with modified time frames. OCC will exercise options automatically if they are in the money at the close on expiration date by at least $0.25 for market maker and firm accounts, and by $0.75 for customer accounts. Clearing members may instruct OCC to exercise options which do not meet these limits or not to exercise options which do.[7]

CUSIP Numbers

Most firms which use CUSIP numbers in standard option record keeping use a six digit root — the assigned CUSIP number — and append an additional three character code to identify the option. Most firms also use this convention for Equity FLEX options.

Symbols

For purposes of clearing, settlement, and back office procedures, a unique format will be used for Equity FLEX symbols on trade match reports and OCC clearing tapes. The symbol will be six characters in length and will adhere to the following convention:

> *Position 1*: 1 or 2, for American Exercise or European Exercise, respectively.
> *Positions 2-4*: Underlying security symbol (AAQ for Apple, MO(blank) for Philip Morris, etc.).
> *Positions 5-6*: The expiration day (e.g., 08 for options expiring on the 8th of the month).

On the OCC tape, the expiration month and year are reported in the same fields as standard options, and the month code will be the same as for standard options. However, the strike price code always will be "Z" and the strike price will be indicated in a separate numeric field.[8]

---

[7] Detailed information is available from the OCC help desk at 1-800-544-6091. An Exchange member intending not to use standard "exercise by exception" processing at OCC must submit a Contrary Exercise Advice notice to the AMEX by 5:30 PM (EST) on expiration day (i.e., the last trading day).

[8] More detailed information is available from the OCC help desk at 1-800-544-6091.

Figure 2: Equity FLEX Large Position Reporting Form

EQUITY FLEX OPTIONS
REPORTING FORM

Firm Name: _____   OCC Clearing Number: _____   Position Date: _____

Prepared By: _____   Telephone Number: _____   Position Type: Customer

                                                                                              Firm

FLEX OPTIONS INFORMATION

Tax I.D./SS#	Account Name/Address	Underlying Stock Symbol	Flex Symbol	Calls (P)uts	Expiration Date	Strike Price	QTY Long	QTY Short

Daily Mark Pricing Practices

The Economic Research Department of the Options Clearing Corporation determines the daily mark price for all FLEX contracts outstanding at the end of a trading day. These mark prices are used by OCC to determine the current value of open option positions, and to set current margin requirements for its member firms. Underlying prices, dividend streams, and interest rate curves are all updated daily. The process for updating implied volatilities is described below. With these updated values, OCC's binomial pricing model produces the daily mark prices.

The updating of implied volatilities involves either interpolation or extrapolation from other similar listed options on the same underlying security. This is performed by generating implied volatility curves across strike prices and covering various maturity bands for both FLEX and standard options on each available underlying security.

Any FLEX product that trades or has a request for quote during a day is used to provide updated points along the FLEX implied volatility curves by implying the volatility from the trade or quote price, using underlying prices from the time of the trade or quote. At the end of the day, new FLEX implied curves will be generated given the updated observations. Thus, new trades or quotes on particular FLEX contracts are reflected in the pricing of other FLEX contracts on a daily basis.

Absent any new FLEX trades or quotes, FLEX implied volatility curves will be updated based on reference to the listed implied volatility curves from each day and any normal spread between the FLEX and listed implied volatility curves that has been observed over time. Any changes in the implied volatilities of the listed options are reflected in FLEX contracts on a daily basis. Any extrapolation significantly beyond the maturities of listed options will generally be trended toward the long-run historical average volatility observed for an underlying security.

Daily mark prices are available from OCC's Options News Network (ONN) or via OCC's daily fax service.[9]

---

[9] The following OCC Economic Research Department telephone numbers may be useful for information regarding FLEX pricing issues, including requests to be added to the daily price fax service: (312) 322-4809; (312) 322-6229; (312) 322-1822; (312) 322-6288.

Figure 3: Flow Chart of Equity Flex Mechanism

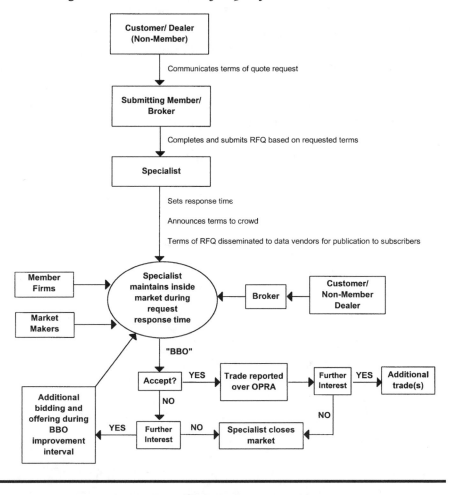

Summary

Figure 3 summarizes the Equity FLEX procedures in a flow chart format.

AMEX Customer Transaction Fees and Options Clearing Corporation Fees

There is a cap on the number of options contracts per trade subject to the Exchange option charges listed in Table 6. These option charges will be imposed on customer trades only for the first 2,000 contracts and on member firm proprietary, specialist and market maker trades only for the first 3,000 contracts. The caps will apply to all three Exchange option fees — transaction, option clearance, and option floor brokerage — and will apply to one day's trades of 100 or more contracts per execution on one side of any series executed by one specialist/trader/broker (for one member firm) and cleared by one clearing firm. The cap will also apply to trades of less than 100 contracts that are multiple contra parties to trades of 100 or more contracts. The same fee schedule and cap provision will apply to standard options, LEAPS and FLEX options. (Effective with transactions effected on and after 6/2/97).

Table 7 summarizes the Option Clearing Corporation's option clearing fees which feature both a quantity discount and a cap at 2,000 contracts.

Table 6: Basic Amex Customer Option Transaction Fee Schedule

	Basic Per Contract Charge Per Side			
	Equity Options		Index Options	
Option Price	≥ $1	< $1	≥ $1	< $1
Option Transaction Fee	$0.30	$0.15	$0.40	$0.20
Clearance Fee	0.04	0.04	0.04	0.04
Floor Brokerage Fee	0.03	0.03	0.03	0.03
Basic fee per side	$0.37	$0.22	$0.47	$0.27

Note: These fees are capped at 2,000 contracts. See text.

Table 7: OCC Clearing Fees for Established Products

Cleared trades of:	Clearing fee (per side):
1 to 500 contracts	$0.09 per contract
501-1,000 contracts	$0.07 per contract
1,000 to 2,000 contracts	$0.06 per contract
Greater than 2,000 contracts	$110.00 per trade (capped)

Appendix A

Terms Used in Equity FLEX Transactions

BBO Improvement Interval: The period during which Equity FLEX participants may modify the quotes established during an initial Request Response Time to improve the best bid or offer. The BBO Improvement Interval is determined by the specialist and may be open-ended until there is no further interest in the requested market.

Crossing of Trades: Crossing of trades will be handled under rules for standard options — except that a Submitting Member who indicates an intention to cross at the time he submits the RFQ is entitled to at least 25% of the trade on a cross.

Exercise Style: Equity FLEX Options are available with American-style or European-style exercise. American-style options may be exercised on any business day through expiration date. European-style options may be exercised only on expiration date.

Expiration Dates: Equity FLEX Options may expire on any business day up to five years from the trade date so long as the expiration date does not fall on or within two business days of a conventional "third Friday" expiration. If the "third Friday" expiration in September falls on Friday, September 17, for example, FLEX Options could not expire on September 15, 16, 17, 20, or 21. Expiration dates beyond three years from the trade require a ruling by a floor official that there is adequate options liquidity to support that long an option life.

Information Dissemination: Requests For Quotes (RFQs) and transactions, including execution price and size, will be disseminated as Administrative Text Messages (ATMs) over the Options Price Reporting Authority (OPRA) wire. See Chapter 6 for detailed descriptions of these message formats. For purposes of clearing, settlement and back office procedures, unique formats and symbols have been specifically designed for FLEX Options.

Last Trading Day: Equity FLEX Options will trade through their expiration date.

Margin Requirements: The minimum margin required for customer short positions in Equity FLEX options is the same as the margin requirement on standard equity options—the current premium plus 20% of the current notional contract value, less any out-of-the-money amount, to a minimum of the current premium plus 10% of the current notional contract value. Standard and Equity FLEX options on Index Shares benchmarked to broad based indexes are subject to 15% margin rather than 20%. Margin is available for spread, straddle and combination positions involving Equity FLEX options, or Equity FLEX options and standard options, up until the opening of trading two business days prior to the expiration date. The OCC may impose an extra margin requirement on firms carrying large, high-risk positions. As a result, firms may require more customer margin.

Member Eligibility Requirements: All AMEX specialists, registered option traders and floor brokers are eligible to participate in Equity FLEX trading.

Minimum Size: The minimum opening transaction size in a new Equity FLEX options series is 250 contracts or the number of contracts overlying a $1 million position, whichever is smaller. For opening transactions in existing Equity FLEX series, the minimum transaction size is 100 contracts—or 25 contracts in a closing transaction.

Multipliers: The multipliers used for FLEX Options will be the same as those used for standard options, i.e., generally 100 shares of an underlying stock and 100 or 1,000 shares for Index Shares. The multiplier may be greater for shares that have split during the life of an option.

Options Clearing Corporation (OCC): Like all exchange-traded options, Equity FLEX options are issued, guaranteed and cleared by The Options Clearing Corporation, an AAA rated company.

The Options Price Reporting Authority (OPRA): See "Information Dissemination."

Position and Exercise Limits: There are no position and exercise limits on Equity FLEX Options. There are, however, additional reporting requirements for large positions.

Quotes: Quotes may be requested as a price per contract or as a percentage of the underlying stock price.

Reporting Requirements: Each AMEX member must file a report (Figure 2 in Chapter 6) with the Exchange when an account is carrying an Equity FLEX option position in excess of three times the position limit for standardized options on that stock. Based on this report, the OCC will perform a risk evaluation of the account and its position, and may impose additional margin.

Request Response Time: The time interval, in minutes, during which responsive bidding and offering will take place. Under AMEX rules, this interval is to be a minimum of 2 minutes and a maximum of 20 minutes as determined by the specialist in consultation with the submitting member. Members may modify the bid, offer and size of their responsive quotes at any point during the Request Response Time.

Settlement: All Equity FLEX Options contracts are physically settled with delivery of the underlying shares.

Specialist Allocation: Equity FLEX Options are allocated to the specialist units currently trading the corresponding standard equity options.

Specialist Requirements: specialists are not subject to any additional requirements above and beyond current capital requirements.

Spreads: Spreads and other combination trades require separate Requests For Quotes (RFQs) for each leg of the trade. There is a "Spread" indication on each RFQ form, which must be marked for each leg of the trade, linking the RFQs in a single trade. A single RFQ message for a multipart trade will be broadcast over OPRA indicating the terms of the desired spread/combination as a single trade.

Strike Prices: Strike prices may be specified as a stock price level or a percentage or numerical deviation from a closing or intraday price level or on any other reasonable method for deriving a strike price. Strike prices for calls will be converted to the nearest standard strike price interval. Strike prices for puts will be rounded to the nearest eighth.

Trading Hours: Trading in Equity FLEX Options will commence each day at 10:00 a.m., New York time and will continue until 4:00 p.m. The half-hour delay from the standard option opening is designed to reduce OPRA traffic at the opening. Trading hours for Equity FLEX Options are subject to change.

Trade Information Dissemination: The terms of each trade will be disseminated over OPRA by the AMEX FLEX staff.

Trading Rotations: There will be no trading rotations in Equity FLEX Options, either at the opening or close of trading.

Appendix B

When Will It Be Possible to Customize Call Strike Prices?

Most users of Equity FLEX options are puzzled by the fact that they can customize put strikes to the nearest eighth of a point in the stock price while E-FLEX call options can only be created with standardized strikes — typically prices ending in 2½, 5, 7½, or 0. The reason behind this limit on customization is a complex and dysfunctional interaction between the securities laws and the United States tax code. The flexibility promised by Equity FLEX conflicts with a provision of the tax code designed to let individual investors sell slightly in-the-money covered calls (designated in the tax code as "qualified covered calls") without running afoul of the dreaded straddle rule which is designed to limit tax deferral and risk reduction with options. At a modest risk of information overload, a brief explanation is appropriate.

It is a close race between the loss-deferral provisions of the straddle rule and the qualified covered call for the title of most complex option feature of the 1984 tax revision. The purpose of the qualified covered call was to simplify record keeping and tax accounting for most covered call writers while eliminating some obviously tax-oriented transactions.

Qualified covered calls provide a limited exemption from the loss-deferral provisions of the straddle rule. Whereas the straddle rule is designed to discourage complex positions which are primarily tax-motivated, the qualified covered call rules are designed to provide a window in the straddle rules. To extend the analogy, it is easy enough to get through the window, but there is some risk the window will slam shut on your leg.

The seller of qualified covered calls can avoid straddle rule loss deferral if:

1. The underlying stock is purchased before or concurrently with the sale of the qualifying covered calls.
2. The call option is traded on a national security exchange.
3. The call option has more than 30 days to expiration and a striking price not less than "available" striking prices defined in the statute.
4. The investor is subject to capital gain or loss tax treatment on the options (i.e., trader's exemptions cannot apply).

The stock price used in computing the minimum striking price is either the closing price of the stock on the previous trading day or the opening price of the stock on the day the option is sold if the opening price exceeds the previous close by more than 10%.

With the table that appears below, this should be easy enough to manage if an investor just remembers not to sell calls that are too far in-the-money. Actually, there are a few more rules.

1. If the underlying stock is long-term at the time an in-the-money but otherwise qualified covered call is sold, any loss on the call is a long-term loss, but any gain is still a short-term gain.
2. If the stock is not long-term before an in-the-money qualified covered call is sold, the holding period of the stock does not include the period during which the call is outstanding unless the stock is sold at a loss. If the stock is sold at a loss, the holding period includes the time during which the call was outstanding.
3. The loss-deferral rule applies to a qualified covered call transaction in which one side is closed out at a loss in one taxable year, and the other side is closed out at a profit in the subsequent tax year unless the profitable side is held "naked" or, in the case of the stock, subject to another covered call for 30 days after the closing of the loss side.

As an alternative to keeping track of all this, many covered writers sell only at- or out-of-the-money calls and never sell stock positions in January.[1]

---

[1] Gary L. Gastineau, *The Options Manual* (1988), pp. 106-107.

The tax code provision which establishes the qualified covered call sets the provisions of a qualified covered call in terms of the number of available qualified covered call strike prices below the stock price that determines the range of eligible strikes. The tax code provision (Section 1092c) does not discuss what happens if Equity FLEX strikes are available at one-eighth point strike intervals in contrast to the minimum five point strike intervals available in 1984. While the clear intent of the statute was to use standard strikes to determine what transactions meet the qualified covered call rule, the statutory reference is to available strikes. Without a restriction on possible strikes, Equity-FLEX clearly expands the number of available strikes dramatically.

To avoid creating a potential problem for individual investors who rely on the qualified covered call provision, the industry decided at the time Equity FLEX options began to trade in October, 1996 to limit the flexibility of strike price selection on Equity FLEX calls until the tax authorities could issue regulations to eliminate the uncertainty. In the summer of 1998, the Internal Revenue Service proposed a regulation which would exclude Equity FLEX strikes from the determination of qualified covered call eligible strikes. With the possibility of public hearings and other delays, a resolution is unlikely before sometime in 1999. The most likely resolution is that Equity FLEX strikes will not affect qualified covered call eligible strikes and that in-the-money Equity FLEX calls will not be eligible for qualified covered call treatment. When the regulation is effective, flexibility will come at last to Equity FLEX call strike prices. For readers who want to understand the problem underlying this delay in call strike flexibilities more thoroughly, we offer the following sections from the Option Clearing Corporation's excellent booklet, "Taxes & Investing: A Guide for the Individual Investor" published in March 1998. This material, prepared by Richard J. Shapiro, Esq. of Ernst & Young LLP is reproduced with the permission of the Option Clearing Corporation and its member exchanges.

TAX CONSIDERATION OF OFF SETTING POSITIONS AND THE STRADDLE RULE

A straddle for Federal income tax purposes involves the holding of "offsetting positions" with respect to personal property. The concept of offsetting positions for individuals embodies a "substantial diminution of risk of loss" test.

A taxpayer has diminished risk of loss where changes in the fair market value of the positions are reasonably expected to vary inversely. If either position composing the straddle materially diminishes the risk of loss on the other position, it would appear that there is substantial diminution of risk of loss. Risk diminution does not require mutuality.

Once an investor holding two or more positions meets the substantial diminution of risk of loss test, the consequences are as follows:

1. There is a suspension or termination of the holding period during the period of offset.
2. The wash-sale rule applies to defer losses realized on certain straddle positions.
3. No current deduction for losses is allowable to the extent of the unrecognized gain (if any) at the end of the taxable year in "offsetting positions" to the loss position, "successor positions" and "offsetting positions to the successor positions." Deferred losses are treated as sustained in the next taxable year, but they are again deferred to the extent of any offsetting unrecognized gain at the end of such year and not otherwise deferred under the wash-sale rule.

In general, a "successor position" is a position which is on the same side of the market (long or short) as was the original position, which replaces a loss position and which is entered into during a period commencing 30 days prior to and ending 30 days after the disposition of the loss position. However, a position entered into after all positions of a straddle have been disposed will not be considered a successor position.

All carrying charges and interest expenses (including margin) incurred during the period of offset are required to be capitalized and added to the basis of the long position. Such capitalized charges are, however, reduced by dividends received on stock included in the straddle. Such expenses are not deductible but, instead, decrease the potential capital gain or increase the potential capital loss upon disposition.

Stock acquired prior to January 1, 1984 should not be subject to these anti-straddle rules, irrespective of how long the stock may be held by the taxpayer or the nature of any other position held. However, it is possible that the Internal Revenue Service could take a different position.

Stock can be part of, but not all of, a straddle involving offsetting positions. For purposes of the anti-straddle rules, long stock against short stock is not treated as an offsetting position. The constructive sale, wash-sale and short-sale provisions, nonetheless, apply.

The substantial diminution of risk of loss test does not require that offsetting stock positions be of the same issuer (though stock against stock alone is not an offsetting position). As a result, stock of one issuer and options on the stock of another may be viewed as offsetting positions in appropriate circumstances.

In contrast, the concept of "substantially identical" for purposes of the wash-sale and short-sale rules requires that stock and options on stock be of the same issuer.

In general, any offsetting position that includes stock and provides a substantial diminution of risk of loss is subject to the anti-straddle provisions. Exceptions include the "qualified covered call."

QUALIFIED COVERED CALLS

A "qualified covered call" is an exchange-traded call option written on stock held by the investor (or stock acquired by the investor "in connection with" the writing of the option) that results in capital gain or loss treatment to the writer. The call option must have more than 30 days to expiration and a strike price not less than the first available strike price below the closing price of the stock on the day before the option was written.

For an option written with more than 90 days to expiration and with a strike price over $50, the covered call must have a strike price no lower than the second available strike price below the closing stock price on the previous day. It should be noted that different strike price intervals (e.g., $2½ versus $5) may exist among the various listed option stocks for comparably priced stocks.

Table 1: "In-the-Money" Qualified Covered Calls

Previous Day's Closing Stock Price*	Lowest Acceptable Strike Price**
$25 or less More than 30 days to expiration	One strike below previous day's closing stock price (no in-the-money qualified covered call if strike price is less than 85% of stock price).
$25.01 to $60 More than 30 days to expiration	One strike below previous day's closing stock price
$60.01 to $150 31-90 days to expiration	One strike below previous day's closing stock price
$60.01 to $150 More than 90 days to expiration	Two strikes below previous day's closing stock price (but not more than $10 in-the-money)
Greater than $150 31-90 days to expiration	One strike below previous day's closing stock price
Greater than $150 More than 90 days to expiration	Two strikes below previous day's closing stock price

* If the opening price on the day the option is written exceeds the previous day's closing price by more than 10%, then the opening price is used in determining the lowest acceptable strike price.
** Whether a covered call is "qualified" is subject to certain special rules, described below.

If the stock price is $150 or less, a qualified covered call cannot be more than $10 "in-the-money." If the closing stock price on the previous day is $25 or less, the strike price must be at least 85% of the stock price. In all cases, if the opening price of the stock on the day the option is written is greater than 110% of the preceding day's closing price, that opening price, rather than the preceding day's closing price, is used in determining the lowest accept-able strike price for a qualified covered call.

Table 1 may help covered call writers determine which options are qualified covered calls. Even if the stock price/strike rules are satisfied, a call that is not an option to purchase stock acquired by the investor "in connection with" the granting of the option would not be qualified. For example, a call written on October 6, 1997 will not be qualified if the stock is purchased on October 10, 1997.

COVERED CALLS — SPECIAL RULES

The basic thrust of the anti-straddle rules is to prevent mismatching of gain and loss. This is accomplished by requiring loss deferral.

Writing an at-the-money (strike price of call equals the stock price used in determining the lowest acceptable strike) or an out-of-the-money (above-the-market) qualified covered call allows the holding period of the underlying stock to continue. However, an in-the-money qualified covered call suspends the holding period of the stock during the time of the option's existence. Further, any loss with respect to an in-the-money qualified covered call is treated as long-term capital loss, if at the time the loss is realized, gain on the sale or exchange of the underlying stock would be treated as long-term capital gain.

Additionally, when a covered call is disposed at a loss in one year and the stock is still owned on the first day of the subsequent year, there is a requirement that the stock be held an additional 30 days from the date of disposition of the call in order for the covered call to be treated as "qualified" for purposes of the loss deferral rule. Generally, only days on which the stock is held "naked" may be counted in determining whether the 30-day holding period is satisfied. However, for this rule the holding period continues to run while the taxpayer is the writer of qualified covered calls.

Similarly, a covered call is not treated as "qualified" for purposes of the loss deferral rule if the covered call is not held for 30 days after the related stock is disposed of at a loss, where gain on closing the option is included in the subsequent year. This rule applies to positions established after December 31, 1986.

Index

A

Acceptance/avoidance, risk isolation, 28–29
Actual shorts, synthetic shorts comparison, 46–49
Actual stock positions, comparative economics, 50–53
ADM. See Administrative text.
Administrative charge, 47
Administrative text (ADM) message, 73, 74
Administrative Text Messages (ATMs), 83
American exercise, 73, 78
style, 21, 37, 62
American option style, 67
American Stock Exchange (AMEX), 3, 9, 55, 57, 58, 62, 65, 68, 70
customer transaction fees, 81–82
member, 77
rules/procedures, 69, 85
American-style call, 77
American-style exercise, 75, 83
AMEX. See American Stock Exchange.
Angel, James J., 1
Anti-straddle rules, 91, 92
Asset allocation, 11
ATMs. See Administrative Text Messages.
At-the-money, 93
calls, 88
put, 18

B

Bartov, Eli, 36
BBO. See Best bid and offer.
Benchmark index, 13
Benchmark rate, 48
Best bid and offer (BBO), 56, 69
improvement interval, 83
Bid/offer process, initiation, 62–69
Bids, 68
Binomial pricing model, 80
Block trading implementations, 30
Bloomberg, 56, 70
Brigham, Eugene, 33
Broad based indexes, 84
Brokerage charges, 51
Brokerage commissions, 51
Broker/dealers, 28
Buyer strategies, 17–20
Buy-in insurance, 25
Buy-ins, protection, 24–25

C

Call options, 15, 16, 88
Call strikes, 62
prices, customization, 87–93
Capital losses, 29, 90. See also Corporate capital losses.
carry forward, 30

Capital reduction, cost, 11
Capital requirements, 85
reduction, 28
Capitalization stock, 49
Cash commitment, 22
Cash dividend, 33
Cash enhancement opportunity, 52
Cash flows, 37, 43, 44
Cash management, 35
Cash management overlay, synthetic long stock position usage, 21–24
Cash premium, 20
Cash requirements, 22
Chance, Don M., 1
Clearance fee, 9
Clearing fees, 9
Closing price, 92
Closing transaction, 57, 67
Cochran, Thomas N., 31
Cole, Kevin, 33
Collar, 27
Commercial paper, 47–49
Common stock, 35
price movements, 25
Comparative economics. See Actual stock positions; Synthetic stock positions.
Contract type, 67
Copeland, Thomas E., 19
Corporate capital losses, renewal, 29–30
Corporate cash, 33
Corporate stock repurchase programs, 31
reasons, 33–35
Corporations, flexibility, 5
Counterparty risk, reduction, 28
Covered calls, 21, 88. See also In-the-money; Qualified covered calls.
special rules, 92–93
treatment, 62
Credit analysis, 45
Cross trade, 67
CUSIP numbers, 78
Customer margin, 84

D

Daily mark pricing practices, 80–81
Damato, Karen, 21, 22
Davies, Erin, 33
Deep in-the-money put/call, 42
Default insurance, 30
Delta-neutral strategy, 77
DIAMONDS, 1
Differential taxation. See Dividends; Interest.
Dividend distribution, 34
Dividend reinvestment plans (DRIPs), 35
Dividend withholding savings, 21
Dividend withholding tax avoidance, 4

synthetic long position creation, 20–21
Dividend yields, 33
Dividend-paying stock position, 46
Dividends, 90
differential taxation, 45–46
Downside exposure, 17, 18
Downside protection, 26
DRIPs. See Dividend reinvestment plans.

E

Earnings per share enhancement, 35
Economic issues, 49–50
Economic Research Department. See Options Clearing Corporation.
E-FLEX call options, 87
Employee benefits, 35
Employee stock options, 35
Equity FLEX administration/rules, 77–78
Equity FLEX operations guide, 57–82
Equity FLEX options
flexible terms, 7–8, 58–62
no position limits, 8–9
Equity FLEX procedures
introduction, 55–57
summary, 81
Equity FLEX trading, eligible stocks/index shares, 58
Equity FLEX transactions, terms, 83–86
Equity options, 84
Equity positions, 49
Equity swap, 42
Equity-equivalent portfolio, 22
European exercise, 78
style, 21, 37, 62
European expiration, 72
European option style, 67
European put, 39
European-style component options, 43
European-style exercise, 83
Evanson, Paul, 33
Event-specific knowledge/belief, 17
Exchange fee, 9
Exchange floor brokerage fee, 9
Exchange specialist, 8
Exchange transaction charge, reductions. See Transactions.
Exchange-listed options, 9
Exchange-traded call, 19
Exchange-traded equity flex, OTC puts comparison, 37–38
Exchange-traded options, 2, 8, 15, 20, 37
institutional use, 3
market, 5
Exchange-traded puts, 31

95